What You
Need to Know
Before You
Fall in
LOVE

DAVID NICHOLSON, Ph.D.

A
JANET
THOMA
BOOK

THOMAS NELSON PUBLISHERS

Nashville • Atlanta • London • Vancouver

Published in Nashville, Tennessee by Thomas Nelson, Inc., Publishers, and distributed in Canada by Word Communications, Ltd., Richmond, British Columbia.

Some names, places, and events in this book have been altered in order to protect the privacy of the individuals involved. Any case examples presented are composites based on the author's clinical experience with many patients.

Library of Congress Cataloging-in-Publication Data

Nicholson, David, 1957-
   What you need to know before you fall in love / David Nicholson.
      p.   cm.
   ISBN 0-7852-8143-6
   1. Mate selection.   2. Intimacy.   3. Love.   4. Marriage—Religious aspects—Christianity.   I. Title.
HQ801.N52   1995
646.7'7—dc20   94-40598
                                                                              CIP

Printed in the United States of America
5 6 — 00 99 98 97 96

To Cindy, my soul mate

Acknowledgments

About four years ago I met with a group of men and women who were involved in their churches' singles ministries. My purpose was to get feedback on a seminar for singles that I had devised and to see what new ideas they could contribute that might make that seminar more helpful and relevant. The cost to me was minimal (I had to buy them lunch) and their input was valuable. It was that seminar's content that provided much of the material for this book. Those at that lunch were Dwayne Adams, John Neesley, Bret Avlakeotes, Paul Royal, Ed and Fern Childress, and Jim Gerlach. I later got feedback from Steve Cretin, Linda Schwob, Ken Dixon, Larry Mercer, and Paul Peterson, all of whom were in some way associated with their churches' singles or premarital ministries.

I'd also like to thank Irene Swindell of the Minirth Meier New Life Clinic in Richardson, Texas, who typed and retyped and retyped the manuscript. "Reenie," as I affectionately call her, is a very godly woman who humbly and devotedly works hard to glorify her Savior.

Lastly, I'd like to express my appreciation to David Wimbish for all of his excellent work in making this manuscript much more reader friendly than it was in its original form.

Contents

One

Are You Looking for the Love of Your Life?

I t wasn't the worst date of my life.

But then again, it was pretty close.

I was smitten with Cindy, one of the most beautiful girls I had ever seen.

But then again, what really impressed me was her deep, thoughtful spirituality. (I was captivated by her spiritual gifts when I saw her for the first time, in a pink bikini, at the pool party my church youth group held at my house.)

Naturally, I asked her out.

She said yes. But not too far into the date, I began to think that a simple, "No, thank you," would have been much better.

Now, I wasn't any modern-day Casanova. I was young

and had been out on a few dates—but not many—so I wasn't aware at first that the date wasn't going so well. But it soon became apparent that the whole evening was headed for the trash heap.

For one thing, she sat so far away from me in the car that her head was practically pressed against the passenger window. That should have been my first clue.

But I had everything planned so beautifully, and I figured I would win her over before the evening was through. You see, I was taking her to a sad movie, *The Other Side of the Mountain,* in which the hero was destined to die in the end. I had figured a three-hanky movie was a good choice—naturally, she would want to be comforted, which meant there would be a good chance I would get to hold her.

But I knew it was time to head home when, during the sad part of the movie, I gently tried to brush away a tear from her cheek while softly saying, "Don't cry."

Immediately she jerked away, as if burned, and gave me a look that is hard to describe. She glared at me as if she had discovered that I alone was responsible for the breakup of the Beatles.

I didn't try to touch her again. I did take her for dessert on the way home. The ice cream was warmer than she.

Would you ask that girl out again?

I did.

Not only that, I asked her to marry me.

Here's what happened: Our second date was four years later. This time I saw her in a college-age Sunday school class, wearing a dazzling red dress that, once again, attracted me to her spirituality. Seeing her again was more than enough to make me forget our first nightmare of a date, so I asked her out again. Once again, she said yes.

Guess what. We had a great time.

It was easy to be with each other. Conversation came naturally. I felt completely at ease, and I could tell she felt the same. Even the silences felt comfortable.

On the way home, during one of those silences, I reached to take her hand and she gave it to me with a beautiful smile.

I knew at that moment that this could be the start of something special.

From then on, Cindy and I had a wonderful romance, and we were married a few years later. We're still very much in love, and, occasionally, we still laugh about that horrible first date.

Why had that date gone so badly?

Perhaps the timing was wrong.

Maybe I tried too hard.

Of course, it didn't help that her mother really liked me.

But my point is that true love doesn't always come up and hit you between the eyes. Sometimes it takes time. Sometimes it sneaks up on you. And sometimes first impressions couldn't be more wrong.

Since you're reading this book, I assume you're looking for the love of your life. My purpose is to help you learn how to find that person.

Now, in all the years Cindy and I have been married, I've learned quite a bit about love and marriage. For one thing, I have discovered that marriage, as wonderful as it is, is not one prolonged ride on a magic carpet woven out of bliss and dreams come true. I've come to realize that anyone who thinks that a love affair or a marriage between a man and woman is going to be one blissful day after another is going to be sorely disappointed. And there are thousands, maybe even millions, of disappointed people in our world.

Far, far too many people have romanticized, idealistic, and unrealistic notions about love and marriage. Their expectations are too high, their commitments to each other are too shallow, and they are not willing to invest the time and energy that is required to make a relationship stand the test of time. They believe in fairy tales and happily-ever-after, instead of commitment and hard work.

That's really a tragedy: Hard work and strong commitments make those fairy-tale endings (or at least their reasonable facsimiles) come true.

That's why I'm writing this book: I want to see more true-life stories that end with, "And they lived (mostly) happily ever after," and fewer that conclude with, "And so they went their separate ways, bitter and hurt, while their divorce lawyers skipped away merrily."

BEFORE YOU FALL IN LOVE . . .

If you are looking for the love of your life, you need to know some specific things *before* you fall in love. Because if you fall in love with the wrong person, or for the wrong reasons—well, it won't be too late for you to stop, think, and "do the right thing," but it will be a lot harder than it would be had you done things right in the first place!

Let's be honest: Some people have some pretty goofy ideas about love and marriage. They think that when they meet Mr. Right, or Miss Right, bells will ring, fireworks will explode, and the birds will chirp sweetly.

Sorry, folks. This world of ours is not a Walt Disney production.

But, having said that, I hasten to add that if you enter into it with your eyes wide open, if you know what you're doing, love between one man and one woman can be the very greatest of life's experiences!

Now before we go any further, I want to tell you just a little bit about who I am, and why I feel qualified to write a book designed for people who are looking for the love of their lives.

As I've already told you, I'm Cindy's husband. And that's something I'm justifiably proud of.

I'm also a clinical psychologist—and over the last several years, I have counseled dozens of men and women who were passing through various stages of romantic relationships.

Before writing the first word of this manuscript, I also spent several years conducting exhaustive literature reviews, poring over hundreds of research articles and books and attending seminars on relationships led by some of the country's most respected authorities.

It's what I have learned through this research and in working with these people, along with my own personal experience, that I will be sharing with you in this book. I've learned a lot over the years about what works, and what doesn't work. I've learned how to make a good relationship better, how to improve a relationship that isn't as good as it could be, and when to turn around and run in the opposite direction from a relationship that's *never* going to be anything but heartache and trouble.

Now, I've been thinking about it, and I can come up with very few things that are more important than finding the love of your life. I mean, this person is going to spend the rest of life with you. If you buy a pair of shoes and you find out later on they're too tight, you can always take them back. But marry the wrong person, and it's going to keep on hurting day after day after day, probably for the rest of your life.

FIRST, KEEP YOUR EYES WIDE OPEN

In today's society people seem to be waiting longer to get married. And in a way that's good because it means that people are generally waiting until they are more mature, more experienced in the ways of the world, before they enter into the marriage contract.

However, my experience tells me that just because people are waiting until they are older to get married doesn't mean they are investing more time and energy into finding the right mate.

For example, some time ago I talked to a man who had waited until he was thirty to get married. But then, when I asked him how long he knew his wife before proposing to her, his answer was, "Oh, about a month. But I really got to know her in that month."

Yeah . . . right! It takes some people more than a month to decide what kind of car to buy. But in a single month's time, this fellow had made a decision that was going to change his life forever. Actually, this couple walked down the aisle less than three months after their first date. And no matter how well they got to know each other during their two-months plus of dating, it wasn't enough . . . because their marriage was in shambles less than a year later.

What happened was simply that at thirty years of age, this gentleman decided, "The time has come to be married." (Contrary to popular belief, women aren't the only ones who hear the loud ticking of the biological clock!) He wanted a wife and he wanted her as soon as possible. Well, he found one. But from the looks of things, this is definitely not a marriage made in heaven. Two rather lonely people got together for all the wrong reasons, and are finding that the loneliness of being single is much preferable to the loneliness that comes from being married to the wrong person.

Hey—marriage is great, as long as you are prepared and walk into it with both eyes wide open.

But sometimes even when two people have their eyes wide open, looking ahead to marriage (or contemplating making a lasting commitment to each other), can be a very frightening thing.

For example, I've recently been counseling a couple whose names are Brandon and Michelle, two single adults who are very much in love, and whose relationship is a major source of happiness for both of them. Yet they are also very concerned about what the future holds.

These two have a lot going for them. Brandon is thirty-two years old and already a successful advisor, working his way up the corporate ladder in a financial planning firm. He seems to know what he wants out of life, and he's well on his way toward getting it. Michelle, who is three years younger, is making a good salary as a computer analyst. She's bright, articulate, energetic, and pretty. The two of them seem to make a good couple on all accounts.

Michelle and Brandon have been dating steadily for eight months, and they've invested time and energy into getting to know one another. They're obviously in love. But they're scared half to death by the thought of making a long-term commitment.

Why?

Brandon is afraid, first of all, because he knows very well that he never had a good role model for what a marriage should be. Even though his parents divorced more than twenty years ago, he and his brothers still carry some of the scars from the divorce and from their parents' bitter battles, both before and after the divorce.

Meanwhile, Michelle comes from a family where the mother and father believed they should "stay together for the sake of the children," despite repeated infidelities on the part of both spouses. And yet, in doing what they thought was best for their kids, they really did what hurt them. Michelle remembers that when she was a girl her parents were not openly antagonistic toward one another, but they were certainly not warm and affectionate either. Both of them were cold and indifferent—toward each other and toward their children.

And those are the reasons why Brandon and Michelle are so scared. Brandon is afraid of getting involved in a relationship that might disintegrate in an ocean of bitterness. Michelle is afraid of being trapped year after year in a loveless, emotionless iceberg of a marriage.

Both Brandon and Michelle wonder if their love is strong enough to stand up to the stress and strain of life in today's fast-paced, demanding world. Both truly hope that the early foundation they have built for their relationship will stand the test of time, but neither one of them really knows what it takes to build a relationship that will last a lifetime.

Adding to their fears is that they know the cold, hard fact

that around 50 percent of first marriages fail. I say *first* marriages, because the failure rate is even higher for second, third, and subsequent marriages—around 64 percent.

And, as Michelle knows all too well, not all failed marriages end up in divorce court. Some of them just go painfully on and on and on.

No wonder the idea of marriage scares them half to death! And despite my joyful feelings on that sultry June evening in 1983, there was a part of me that was also afraid. There are times I still am because over the years I've come to realize how hard it is to maintain a healthy marriage; I've also seen the marriages of people I dearly love explode with life-wrenching results.

But my experience as a counselor has taught me that there are at least three significant factors that can help you learn how to make the wisest possible choice when it comes to finding *The One*, the person you want to spend the rest of your life with.

These three factors are:

1. The need to acquire an awareness of basic relationship principles; in other words, the need to understand what it is that makes relationships work, and what it is that makes them fail
2. The need to develop an understanding of the dynamics found within our families of origin and our own personalities (please don't be frightened because that sounds kind of "technical" or "clinical;" all it means is that it's just as important to know yourself, who you are, and why you are the way you are, as it is for you to know your loved one)

3. The need to learn how to relate and talk to each other, as well as resolve conflict (and you *will* have conflict to talk through, you know)

This last point is particularly important.

Knowing how to communicate and problem solve is *so* important—and that's why I'll have quite a lot to say on the subject.

Again, I want to help you acquire all this important knowledge *before* you're sitting down with the caterer and planning your wedding reception.

Unfortunately, once a couple is engaged and involved in the process of planning a wedding, a condition known as "brain-lock" sets in. It's easy to see why. Planning a wedding is no small thing. There are invitations to send out, a reception to plan, flowers to order, travel plans to make, and on and on. The months leading up to a wedding can be among the most fearful and pressure-filled in anyone's life. Thus, brain-lock occurs, a condition which is no respecter of a person's usual intellect or clarity of mind.

During the time when he or she is experiencing brain-lock, a person can no longer make rational observations and decisions related to what he or she is doing.

During this period, several obvious facts may emerge which would tell the properly functioning brain, "Hey, you had better think twice about marrying this person." For example, it may be determined during this time that she's very conservative while he's extremely liberal; that she's a morning person while he's a night owl; that she likes solitude while he always wants to be in the middle of a crowd; that she likes the great outdoors but he'd rather stay at home; that she likes to discuss the great issues of the day but he's more comfortable talking about the latest adventures of Calvin and Hobbes!

As I said, if brain-lock were not a factor, recognition of all these facts would cause a couple to say, "Maybe we'd better think twice about this." But because of brain-lock, it's very hard to think twice. Whenever something the least bit "fearful" comes up, they tend to push it back beneath the surface. (Actually, the bustle of wedding preparations isn't the only factor involved here. There's also the matter of, "Hey, I can't look at the situation too closely right now. I mean, what if I find out I really shouldn't be marrying this person? What would I do then? I can't back out now because we've already sent out invitations and given the caterer a deposit!)

I've even had people tell me, "I was walking down the aisle, knowing I was doing the wrong thing . . . wanting to call the whole thing off . . . but I was trapped."

That's certainly not a very good way to start a marriage, and you don't have to be a Ph.D. to figure that out.

Now before we go any further, let me assure you that I don't believe that picking "the love of your life" should be a cold, calculating, sterile process. This is not the sort of thing where you line up the pros on one side of a paper, the cons on the other side, and make your decision based on whether there are more positives or negatives.

I believe in love. I believe it is one of God's great gifts to humankind. I believe there is very little in this world that can be as beautiful as a man and woman who are deeply, truly, and everlastingly in love with one another. But I also believe in being wise and knowledgeable, and I do not buy the notion that "love is blind."

It may be true, as The Beatles sang, that "All you need is love." But the love we're talking about must be based on a whole lot more than mutual physical attraction, a neurotic "need" for another person, or upon a desire for companionship. True love, the type discussed in the thirteenth chapter of 1 Corinthians, can withstand close examination. If it's really love you feel, looking at it closely will only serve to make it stronger.

A few years ago, Michael Martin Murphy had a hit song called "What's Forever For?" You may remember the question asked in the lyrics of this song, "If love never lasts forever, tell me, what's forever for?"

Well, love *can* last forever—but sometimes it needs some help, especially in this hectic, dangerous age. Marriage has never been a cakewalk, but the pressures of our times can turn it into a death march over hot coals. It doesn't have to be that way. And I don't want it to wind up being that way for you.

WHAT I WANT TO GIVE YOU

In our journey together through this book, I want to:

- Give you some practical advice that is designed to help you find the person you want to share your life with
- Tell you how you can go about the process of finding and building a love that will last
- Help you recognize your motives for entering into a romantic relationship (this is important so that you can act on the healthy motives, and refuse to be swayed by the unhealthy ones)

- Discuss the dynamics of a healthy relationship: what it looks like, what it feels like, and how those involved within it relate to each other
- Talk about the importance of understanding your family background as well as your loved one's family background
- Give you some tips about effective communication— which is so important to any interpersonal relationship

I'm not really interested in giving you abstract theories. I want to give you practical advice and suggestions that are going to work for you. And because I want this book to be as helpful as it can possibly be, I'm also going to give you addresses and phone numbers of various organizations that can assist in different areas of "relationship construction and maintenance."

So . . . are you ready?

It's time to start out on our journey, looking for, and building, that love that will last a lifetime.

Coming up next, a look at why people fall in love.

Let's go!

Two

Why People Fall in Love

Late one starlit Friday evening, Jimmy and Sandi were walking hand-in-hand through the darkened atrium of a mostly deserted mall. They had just taken in a romantic movie and were enjoying a wonderful moment together.

Jimmy and Sandi were in love with a capital L. They were walking through the mall, but they were so much in love that they might as well have been walking through the *Champs-Élysées* in Paris. What made this time even more exciting was that three weeks earlier, Jimmy had eagerly offered and Sandi had just as eagerly accepted his marriage proposal. Now, in the wake of that happy moment and prior to all the hassles and headaches involved in planning the typical American mega-wedding, the blissful couple was in a particularly playful mood.

Sandi began by coyly asking, "And, so, Mr. Jenkins—if

that's your real name—why is it exactly that you want to marry me?"

Surprisingly quick in his retort, the usually quiet Jimmy countered, "You know . . . I've been devoting a lot of thought to that question recently, and . . . for the life of me, I have absolutely no idea."

Of course, this response provoked immediate laughter as the two carried on much in the way small children do when they are absolutely lost in play. A nearby security guard turned from his typically boring routine to look at the lovers, and smiled knowingly.

After regaining their dignity and their stride, Jimmy returned to her question, but this time more seriously than before. "Because," he told her, "you are everything I've ever wanted in a wife."

Gazing intently into her eyes he continued, "I have thought for a long time that in order for me to be happy—I mean *really* happy I needed to have a partner: a woman who loved only me. A woman who thought I was really neat and who would cherish and love me as much as I loved and cherished her." He paused, and then, in his best Bogart impersonation, added, "And, shweetheart . . . you just happen to fit the bill."

Sandi stood on her tiptoes, gently pressing her cheek to his, and whispered, "Great answer. Bad Bogey."

Jimmy had answered from his heart, and every word he spoke was true. Furthermore, the reasons he gave were all valid, healthy reasons for deciding on a life partner. But Jimmy is no exception to the truth that all of us have healthy and unhealthy parts to our personalities. And many times in life our motivations are mixtures of the positive and the negative. What he did not share, and probably was not even fully aware of, were some of the less-healthy reasons why he had fallen in love with Sandi, and why he wanted to marry her.

WHY DO PEOPLE FALL IN LOVE?

How do people decide with whom they are going to spend the rest of their lives? Is there any way to ensure that you're doing it for the right reasons instead of the wrong ones? What are the right reasons anyway? And what are the wrong ones?

I'm convinced that if you were to stop a dozen married people on the street and ask them why they got married, chances are very good that almost all of them would tell you that it was because they were "in love." But if you were able to dig a little deeper beneath the surface and get more reasons, I'd also be willing to bet that people really paired off for reasons like the following ones:

- They didn't want to be alone
- They wanted someone to take care of them
- They wanted to get away from their parents
- That old biological clock was ticking like crazy, and it was now or never
- Their hormones were boiling like a sidewalk in Phoenix in the middle of August
- It was what other people expected them to do

Most of the time, we fall in love with a member of the opposite sex because of a combination of things. For example, we are attracted to people whose looks we like. We may deny that and say that physical appearance doesn't really have anything to do with it—but it almost always does.

Would it be healthy to marry someone simply because you liked their looks? Of course not. And yet that's one of the factors that almost always enters into the process of "falling in love." We tend to judge people, at least initially, by their looks.

In addition to being classified as "healthy" or "unhealthy," motives for falling in love and/or getting married can be divided into three distinct categories: intrinsic, instrumental, and external.

Intrinsic motives have to do with "who we are as a couple," the essential and defining qualities of "us." In other words, some of the intrinsic reasons you fall in love with someone may include because you are close and intimate with him or her, because the two of you have become truly devoted to each other, or because you feel more whole and complete within your partnership with that other person.

Instrumental motives are those associated more with what the other person can do for *you.* This sounds selfish, and sometimes it is, but not always. The truth is, very rarely will a person fall in love with someone who never does anything for them. It has happened that, for whatever reasons, some people have fallen in love with others who were mean, abusive, and selfish, who never had a thought for anyone but themselves. But usually that is born only out of a psychological need to be abused. Almost all of us expect to get *something* out of the person with whom we fall in love.

External motives are the least personal, and often have nothing at all to do with your own desires or feelings toward the other person. For example, you may decide that you want to be with another person simply because he or she is someone your parents approve of. That's an external motive. Studies have found that when one partner in a relationship has strong external reasons for being together, but the other person doesn't, their chances of splitting up increase. I'm sure you can see that most of the unhealthy reasons for falling in love and getting married fall into this last classification.

Now let's get specific, and talk about some of the unhealthy reasons why people choose their lifetime partners. And as we do, please examine yourself as closely as you can to see if any of them apply to you. It may be painful to see that they do. But believe me . . . it is better to have a little pain right now that causes you to make the right decision than to make a wrong decision and to suffer for it your entire lifetime.

THINK-AGAIN REASONS FOR FALLING IN LOVE

What are some of the wrong reasons people use for getting involved in romantic relationships? We'll discuss some of the more common reasons below.

Rebounding

It's dangerous to rush into a new relationship when you've just ended an old one. This is especially true if it wasn't you who wanted to end the old one. People who have been, pardon the expression, dumped, are particularly susceptible to getting seriously involved with someone new for all the wrong reasons.

For example, they may want to prove to the person who dumped them that *somebody* loves them. They may want to prove it to themselves, too. And in that state of mind, they are willing to overlook a whole bunch of warning signals that this relationship may not be the best thing for them. It's hard to believe, I know, but I've even been dumped a time or two myself. And you know what? Today, I'm grateful (sort of) for every one of those dumpings!

Anyway, it is true that, as the wise old philosopher Neil Sedaka sang in the early 1960s, "Breaking up is hard to do." If there was any depth at all to a relationship, a breakup will leave the person who has been "dumped" reeling. His or her self-esteem will be damaged, he or she will probably be left with feelings of insecurity, and, of course, there will be emotional pain to deal with. All of these things combine to make this person extremely vulnerable to a "rebound relationship."

What's so bad about a rebound relationship? The biggest problem is that the emotional pain and vulnerability you're experiencing might lead you to enter into another relationship without giving it sufficient forethought or caution.

It's often a matter of, "I've been hurting so badly, and I just need someone to hold me for a little while." There is also the feeling that, "Gee, this person I really cared about left me, so I must not be worth very much. I guess I'll have to lower my standards." And another thing is that it is easy to mistake feelings of appreciation or sympathy for love . . . and that's true for both parties. You might think you love someone when you're really just grateful for the attention he or she has shown you, or else you're feeling sorry for someone because he or she is nursing a broken heart.

Another reason some people get involved in rebound

relationships is because they have been comfortable as part of a couple, and they're not used to being on their own. They feel like they just have to be with somebody, and as soon as one relationship ends, they're looking around anxiously for the next one. Watch out for these people. They are dangerous!

The best thing to be said about rebound relationships is that you should leave them to the National Basketball Association. If you've had your heart broken, give it some time to heal. And be careful of anyone else who might be on the rebound.

Once your self-image has begun to recover and you're seeing the world through normal eyes, that's the time to think about serious dating again. Otherwise, you may "come to your senses" when it's much too late. You're likely to find yourself attached to someone you never would have considered if you were in your "right" state of mind.

Here are some questions to ask yourself to avoid getting entangled in a rebound relationship:

- Was I, or the person I'm dating, recently dumped before we began to get involved?
- How much time has passed since the breakup of the previous relationship (either yours or your date's)?
- How serious was the previous relationship? (The deeper the previous relationship, the more time it will take to get over it; it is also true that a breakup of a serious relationship will hurt more, and be more likely to send the "dumpee" running into the arms of someone else)

- Do I really love this person or is he or she simply an antidote to my pain?
- What is it about this person that makes me feel about him, or her, the way I do?

If you or your partner had recently been "dumped" before you got together, it would be a good idea to take a good, hard look at your relationship. It's unwise to enter into a new relationship before the scars left from the breakup of an old relationship have healed—and this will generally take a minimum of several weeks, and sometimes several months.

Rebellion

Most of us take part in small acts of rebellion, and that's no problem. But it can be a whale of a problem if you get involved in a romantic relationship with someone just because other people object to him, or her.

We might consider this "attraction through rebellion" to be "The Romeo and Juliet Phenomenon," in which the attraction between two people is significantly increased because of the disapproval of one or both sides of parents. Social science research has actually borne this out in studies that have shown how parental interference can actually increase feelings of romantic attraction between partners.

The basic problem with this type of relationship is that it hasn't developed on its own merit, nor will it stand on its own. It occurs primarily because of what some non-involved party (in most cases, the parents) thinks or wants, instead of what the two partners want or think about each other. Remember that we talked about external motives and said that they are the worst reasons for getting married . . . and this is one of the worst external motives.

You've heard of cutting off your nose to spite your face? This is like cutting off your nose, your ears, and your lips to spite your face. Don't do it! It will hurt you (or at least your face) far worse than it will hurt anyone else.

The main problem here, though, is that it's difficult to stop and ask yourself a question like, "Would I really love this person as much if everyone I know was in favor of our relationship?"

The person who is getting involved romantically because of rebellious motives is saying to his partner, in effect: "I am not choosing you mainly because I'm attracted to your qualities. I choose you because my parents (or others) are against this whole idea, and I'm going to show them that I'm big enough and strong enough to make my own decisions, even if it means throwing my life away by committing myself to someone like you."

It's true that people who tend to marry out of rebellion are often teenagers, but that may be in terms of emotional maturity, not chronological age. Either way, they haven't developed their own individuality in a healthy way and are using marriage to prove that they are "grown up."

Here are some questions to ask yourself if you think that you might be getting involved in a relationship based on rebellion:

- How opposed are my parents, or my partner's parents, to this relationship?
- How different is my partner from my parents' values, ideals, and expectations?
- Does either my partner or I get some satisfaction from

the fact that our parents disapprove of our relationship but can do nothing to stop it? To what degree do I have the attitude of "I'll show them"?

- If our relationship ended, to what degree would I be hesitant to let my parents know about it because I wouldn't want them to have the satisfaction of thinking that they were "right all along"?

Rebellion may not be the *major* reason you and your partner are together. But if your answers to the above questions show you that it is certainly an important part of the relationship, then I suggest you rebel against your rebellion. Call the whole thing off and do it now!

Escape

Thousands of people get married every year for no other reason than that they're trying to escape an unpleasant situation. These people are almost always very young—the majority from sixteen to nineteen years of age—and they are frequently victims of physical, sexual, or emotional abuse. It is also often true that they are the oldest of many brothers and sisters and are marrying to get out of a parenting role that has been thrust upon them against their will. They see getting together, and perhaps getting married, as their only "legitimate" ticket out of a difficult situation. But unfortunately, the person who is escaping often runs into a situation exactly like or even worse than the one he left behind.

For a dramatic example of this, take a trip to the mountains of eastern Kentucky or the slums of Detroit. There you will find hundreds of desperately poor young couples—kids of no more than fifteen or sixteen, already with

one or two children. They have very little education, virtually no skills, and no hope for a better future. Why did they
marry? To escape the poverty and deprivation of their
parents' homes. But instead of escaping, they have merely
succeeded in duplicating the conditions they were trying
to leave behind. The cycle will be repeated for years to
come, and it's a terrible tragedy.

Yes, I realize that is a dramatic example, but it is true
that people who fall in love and cling to each other because
they are trying to escape some situation or other are almost
always headed for trouble.

Once again, as is true of the "rebel" relationship, an
"escape" relationship happens for indirect reasons—not
because "You have all the qualities I would like to have in
a partner," but because "You can help me escape an
intolerable situation." It is also true that the person who is
trying to escape from a bad home life probably hasn't had
very good role models with regard to male-female relationships.

The majority of these people aren't even close to being
able to function in a mature, mutually giving way in a
relationship. They can barely take care of themselves, and
they're in no position to face the trials and challenges that
are needed to construct a lasting relationship.

Are you looking for love as a means of escape? If you
think you might be, ask yourself these questions:

- How pleasant has my home life been?
- How strongly do I feel compelled to "get out" of my
  parents' home?
- Have I or my partner been emotionally, physically, or
  sexually abused?

- Have I or my partner ever lived independently outside of our parents' homes?

If honesty compels you to admit that your home life was never very good and that you couldn't wait to be old enough to escape it, if you or your partner has ever been abused, and if neither one of you has ever lived independently by yourself, please think very seriously about ending the relationship. Only you can truthfully see the reasons why you "fell in love" with this person, but if an honest examination of the situation reveals that it has more to do with your parents and your life with them than it does with him or her—it's time to apply the brakes. Otherwise— well, have you ever heard of jumping from the frying pan into the fire?

It's important to remember that while some people have a need to escape, there are others who have a need to rescue. These people often confuse love and sympathy, or else they rescue because it's a way they can be needed by someone else. Whatever the motive, a marriage based on an escape-rescue type of relationship is not likely to last.

Because you want to escape something, or because you want to rescue someone, is no reason at all to enter into a romantic relationship.

Physical Appearance

At the risk of being utterly profound, let me tell you that initial attraction to a person of the opposite sex is almost always based on physical appearance. We all want to be with someone we like to look at, and that we're proud of. And we all want to look as good as we possibly can.

But just the same, any relationship that is based primarny on physical attraction is likely to be a short-term affair. After all, physical beauty is pretty much the province of the young. As we get older, we begin wrinkling, sagging, graying, balding, and "pooching out" in areas where we shouldn't "pooch out." A friend of mine used to explain this phenomenon by shaking his head sadly and saying that he had "Dunlaps" disease. Then, whenever a sympathetic stranger asked him what this meant, he'd reply, "It means that my stomach done laps over my belt."

Anyway, and despite the way most of us seem to think about it, there is an old saying that mothers have been repeating to their little girls almost since the beginning of time: "Pretty is as pretty does." Yes, that's an old cliché, but it's also true. We've all known people we thought were quite attractive, but who, as we got closer to them and saw that their actions weren't so "pretty," began to lose their physical allure. And then, most of us have also had friends who may not have been all that attractive from a purely physical standpoint, but who were so nice and so pleasant that the closer we got to them the better looking they became. Appearances can be deceiving.

Is physical appearance too important to you? Here are some questions to ask yourself:

- How important to me is it that others think my boyfriend or girlfriend is good-looking?
- How jealous do I want people to feel when they see me with my partner?
- To what degree does my partner's physical appearance influence my overall attraction toward him or her? Do my feelings toward my partner fluctuate with regard to how good he or she looks at the moment?

If you answered the first question by saying that it is very important to you that others think your partner is good-looking, that alone is reason to rethink the relationship. Liking someone's looks is a very shallow reason for entering into a relationship, and it's not likely to be a lasting one or a fulfilling relationship. And if you go out with your boyfriend or girlfriend because you want other people to be jealous of you—well, that's even worse. Not much hope for a long-lasting, satisfying relationship there. And regarding the final question—if your feelings toward your partner seem to fluctuate with how good he or she looks at the moment . . . well, that isn't love!

Now please don't think I'm saying that just because the woman you love is stunningly beautiful, or because the guy you're going with is gorgeous, the relationship can't work. There's nothing at all wrong with loving someone who is attractive, *unless* that's your sole or primary reason for loving that person.

Another wrong reason why people get together is because they're just plain tired of being alone.

Loneliness and Unhappiness

We sometimes think that being with someone—anyone—would be better than being by ourselves.

The book of Proverbs has some good advice: Namely, that it's better to live alone in a tiny attic than to share a palace with an unpleasant wife or husband. In other words, being lonely by yourself can be preferable to being lonely *with* another person. Some people even feel sadder and more alone after "falling in love" because they find that it isn't the end-all to their problems that they thought it was going to be.

I remember talking to one young man who knew that he wasn't treating his girlfriend right. He was short-tempered and sarcastic with her, and naturally this was causing trouble between them. He said, "I know I'm not being fair, but I thought she was going to make me happy, and it just hasn't happened."

All I could say to him was that if he was depending on another person to make him happy, then he was definitely looking for trouble. To put it as simply as possible, your happiness shouldn't depend upon anyone but you.

If you are chronically unhappy, you need to spend some time getting to know why. It might be a very good idea to seek out a therapist. It's usually true that if a person generally feels lonely and unhappy when he is by himself, he will continue to feel lonely and unhappy when he's part of a couple.

Here are some questions to help see if you're in danger of making this mistake:

- How lonely and unhappy was I before I became involved with my partner?
- How lonely and unhappy am I now when my partner is not around?
- How difficult is it for me to be alone?
- How hard do I strive to avoid this?
- Do I like myself?

I realize that these aren't the easiest questions to answer. It's hard to admit that the problem may lie within you, rather than be the result of something you're missing—such as a loving boyfriend or girlfriend. But it's better to recognize that what you need may be some sessions with a good counselor rather than jumping into a relationship with someone who is given the unreasonable task of making you happy.

"Okay . . . now make me happy!" That's too much to ask of anyone.

Because You Are Co-Dependent

Okay, I admit it. Co-dependency was one of the buzzwords of the 80s—something of a fad. Having said that, I also have to say that co-dependency can be a very real problem. One common characteristic of co-dependency is the desire to be a caretaker or to rescue others from their various emotional problems, ills, etc. Thus, a co-dependent relationship can result when one of the partners perceives the other to be somehow less competent, less capable, weaker, and more needy. The co-dependent partner wants to be desperately needed and feels that the other person needs him or her desperately. Often, this person wants to terminate the relationship, but can't, because of the fear that his or her partner just wouldn't be able to get along without them.

Sometimes, this person is held captive by comments like: "I just couldn't live without you," or even, "If you leave me, I'll kill myself !"

If you are involved in a relationship with someone who says things like that, I've got a very good piece of advice: Put on your Reeboks and run like crazy in the opposite direction!

Oh, I realize that it's normal for people in a relationship to say things like, "I need you," and "I couldn't live without you," but what I'm talking about here goes much deeper than ordinary "love talk." If you're involved in a co-dependent relationship, get out of it before it's too late!

Below are some questions to ask yourself to see if you might be in danger of getting involved in a co-dependent relationship:

- Do I see myself as significantly stronger than my partner emotionally and psychologically?
- Do I see my partner as having substantial emotional problems?
- Do I think my partner would have a hard time making it in life without my help?
- Do I feel obligated to help my partner overcome his or her problems?
- What do I think would probably happen to my partner if I ended this relationship?

If you answered yes to the first four questions, and if your answer to the fifth question is less than positive, then it's probably time to lace up those tennies and start running!

Social Pressure

This is especially true for women, who usually have a great deal of prodding from moms, aunts, grandmothers, and assorted other women to "find a nice young man." If a woman reaches her mid-twenties without having someone "serious" in her life, she's likely to prefer Chinese water torture to those family reunions where Aunt Agnes chases her all over the place, showing her pictures of every "nice young man" she's ever met—from stockbrokers to stock boys, and including her next-door neighbor, Bernie, who's still decked out in a lime green leisure suit and weighed down by a dozen or more gold chains.

Funny, isn't it? Some of these older women may have terrible marriages. They have husbands who don't pay any attention to them, who are tight as can be with a dollar, and who snore *loudly*. But they still want the young women in their families to find a guy and get married. Strange, indeed.

Another form of social pressure takes place when your friends are pairing off and taking that trip down the aisle. The unattached person begins to feel like a "fifth wheel" in social situations.

Here are some questions to ask yourself to see if your desire for romance has been brought about primarily by social pressure:

- Do I feel odd being "unattached" at my age?
- Are there subtle or overt pressures from friends and relatives for me to find that "special someone"?
- Have I been made to feel that I will "lose my chance" if I don't find someone right away?
- Have I been made to feel that my still being single is a disappointment to my parents?

The only reason to enter into a relationship is because you've found someone you really want to be with, not because others tell you that you *need* to find somebody. If you've answered yes to two or more of these questions, then it's time to stop listening to others, to stop worrying about what *they* think, and spend some time listening to your own heart.

Financial or Personal Gain

I really don't feel the need to say very much about this. But it can be tempting to settle for money when you've had a difficult time finding love.

And, sometimes, there can be the tendency to want to hold on to someone just because he (or she) can improve your status in life.

"Well, I'd be crazy to let him go. He's so sophisticated. He comes from a good family. He speaks three languages. He's got plenty of money. And he's got a tremendously bright future ahead of him."

"Do you love him?"

"Well, no. But I could *learn* to love him."

Don't bet on it.

If you are a divorced or widowed mother of small children, this may be an especially difficult temptation, because you want someone who will help you take care of your children. While that's understandable, it's always a mistake to throw all other considerations to the wind and enter into a serious relationship because you will benefit financially or socially.

Ask yourself these questions:

- How significant will the economic advantages be if I stay with this person?
- Would I still want to be with this person if he (she) suddenly suffered a financial setback?
- How important is money to me?
- Would I still want to be with this person if he (she) was no better off financially than I am?

If you can see that you really wouldn't want to be with this person if he or she didn't have money, then you're better off breaking up now. There are better and easier ways to make your fortune than to spend the rest of your life locked in a loveless and emotionally unfulfilling relationship—like prospecting for gold in Arizona's Superstition Mountains, or earning fame and fortune by riding bucking broncos and wrestling steers in the rodeo!

Because You're in Love with Love

Before we move on, a few words of warning are in order, about a most confusing and sometimes devious thing: A thing called romance.

Someone says, "What do you mean romance is devious? Romance is wonderful!"

Yes, but it can also get you into lots and lots of trouble. Let me explain.

Have you ever been so much in love that you just sort of drifted through your day in a state of bliss? You know what I mean? There is a euphoria that comes with falling in love, with walking hand-in-hand on moonlit beaches, with romantic dinners eaten in candlelight, with deep sighs and lingering kisses.

During the time when you've first fallen in love, no matter how hard you might try, you just can't seem to get your feet on the ground. You don't walk, you float. You think the world and everything in it is just wonderful, and if it weren't for the fact that other people know what it's like to be in love, they might call the men in white coats to come take you away.

Well, the truth is that romance can be a wonderful thing, but it can also be a blinding thing. It can cover a multitude of sins and blemishes.

This is the primary reason why you should never, never,

never marry someone until you've really taken the time to get to know them. Those who float into marriage dancing on a cloud of romantic ecstasy are almost always going to wind up disappointed. After a while, the drug of romance begins to wear off, and Snow White and Prince Charming are left staring at each other in disbelief. She's thinking, "What happened? I thought I was marrying the prince, and instead I wound up with one of the Seven Dwarfs—Grumpy!" And he's wondering how his "beautiful princess" could have transformed so quickly into the "Evil Queen."

Now for a relationship to be optimally healthy there has to be romance and lots of it. But just the same, if a couple decides to marry while they are still in the initial "romance is everything" stage of their relationship they are setting themselves up for a lot of pain and trouble later on.

Some people are flat-out "in love with love." They are what you might call "romance junkies," and as soon as the euphoria begins to fade, they're ready to scrap the relationship and move on to the next one. But you can't build a solid, lasting relationship on romance alone.

If you can't think of a single flaw in your boyfriend's or girlfriend's character, or anything about them that even occasionally bugs you, then you're probably still floating around in a romantic haze. After all, everyone has some character flaws, and one or two little habits that tend to be irritating. The romantic haze period of a relationship can be quite enjoyable. But just don't decide on something as important as marriage until you are able to make an objective assessment of the strengths and weaknesses of your relationship—romance notwithstanding.

Have I told you about Jean Arthur and Julian Anker? In

twenty-four hours, they got married *and* divorced. That's got to be a record. The cloud of romance doesn't usually dissipate quite so quickly. At the same time, though, it is true that reality does eventually intrude into the most romantic relationships.

Now, at last, let's move on to a healthy and good reason why men and women pair off.

SOME GOOD REASONS FOR FALLING IN LOVE

For Companionship

Every one of the five billion people on this planet has a need to connect intimately with at least one other human being. It is natural and healthy to want to love and be loved by a journey mate who will share life's ups and downs as a beloved companion. The need to develop an emotional closeness with another person is an ingrained part of every healthy individual. In other words, that's the way God made us.

If you'll get your Bible and turn to the first two chapters of Genesis, you'll find an account of God's creation of the universe. And you'll see that after every specific act of creation, God was pleased and felt that things were "good." The only time He felt that things weren't good was when He saw that man was alone. In fact, He said it straight out: "It is not good that man should be alone" (Gen. 2:18).

Does that mean you can't be happy unless you're connected to another person? I wouldn't go that far. But I would say that it means you cannot be *optimally* happy without some sort of intimate relationship. In the same way, no human being can be *optimally* happy, peaceful, or joyful without an intimate relationship with the Creator.

Because You Want to Have a Family

The desire to have children, to fulfill a parenting role, and to help instruct future generations can be a *part* of one's healthy motivation to find a life partner. However, if this is the sole motivation, or even the primary motivation, it can become a negative. At that point, you're no longer choosing the other person because of who he or she is, but because you want to use them to achieve your own goal—having children.

Just the same, the desire to have children is something God has built into us. Again turning to the first chapter of Genesis, verse 28, we find the Lord telling the first man and woman on earth to "be fruitful and multiply." Turning over to the ninth chapter, verse one, we find God giving the same command to Noah and his family after the Great Flood. Someone has said that the birth of a baby is an expression of God's opinion that the human race should continue. I believe that's true. God is pro-children. I think that is obvious not only through the words of the Bible, but through the fact that He designed it so that children are brought into the world through the loving, intimate act of sexual union between a man and a woman. True sexual intimacy between two people who deeply love each other is, in my opinion, the most pleasurable experience available to mankind. And if you stop and think about it for a moment, I'm sure the fact that God uses such a wonderful experience to bring children into the world will strike you the way it strikes me—as truly amazing.

Most human beings, women *and* men, have a desire for family, and it's a desire that is God-given.

Still another good reason for getting involved in a relationship is . . .

For Emotional Security

There's nothing at all wrong with the desire for a secure relationship with someone who will share his or her lifetime with you—someone who will always be there for you when you need someone to lean on, to talk to, to cry with or laugh with. Someone who will not only love you through all the storms of life, but who will also be there for you to love.

Things change rapidly in this world of ours. Sometimes, too rapidly. Friends move in and out of our lives. Loved ones grow old and die. Things that we thought would last forever crumble into so much dust and dirt.

That's one of the reasons why there is so much comfort in God's promise that He is the same "yesterday, today, and forever." There is great security in God's constancy, and there is the same sort of security in a loving relationship in which both partners cling tightly to each other no matter what!

I realize that I have spent most of my time in this chapter talking about negative reasons for entering into a relationship or getting married. That's because getting involved with someone or marrying someone for the wrong reason can bring you tremendous hurt and pain. But, on the other hand, there is very little in this life that can compare with the wonderful joy and happiness that comes from finding the person you're going to love for the rest of your life.

Yes, there are great risks here, but they are risks worth taking.

Next up, we'll discuss some lies that people tend to tell themselves about love, engagement, and married life that can be setups for misery.

Three

Love Lies: Myths About Engagement and Marriage

W hat old song says it's a sin to tell a lie?

The funny thing is that even though we know it's wrong, most of us still tell a lie from time to time. At least a little bitty one. If true life were patterned after fairy tales, it would be easy to spot the *real* liars among us. They would be the ones who keep getting their noses slammed in the door. (You do remember what happened to Pinocchio, don't you?)

But it's just not that way and, unfortunately, almost all of us have fallen victim to liars at one time or another. Oh, maybe we haven't driven off the lot with a car that was "owned by a little old lady from Pasadena who just drove it to church on Sunday," only to have the transmission fall out at the first stoplight. Maybe we haven't bought some "beautiful waterfront property" in Florida, only to find out that the land was covered with water. But we've all believed a thing or two we shouldn't have believed!

Part of the problem is that it's often easier to believe a lie than to accept the truth. As Henry David Thoreau said, "It takes two to speak the truth—one to speak and another to hear" (*Bartlett's Familiar Quotations*. Boston: Little Brown & Co., 1980).

If you lie to people and they catch you, it will make them angry, distrustful, and it may mean the end of a friendship.

So it is not wise to lie to anyone—including yourself. In fact, if you do tell yourself lies, it can make you downright crazy!

Psychologist Chris Thurman discusses this in his book *The Lies We Believe* (Nashville: Thomas Nelson Publishers, 1989). Dr. Thurman says that many of the emotional and mental disorders that people experience can be attributed to lies they believe about the world, life, themselves, and God. Believing these lies creates negative emotions that add unnecessary suffering to our lives.

He goes on to identify several lies that he believes contribute to conflict and disharmony between partners.

Dr. Lawrence Kurdek of Wright State University has also done research which found that couples in which either partner holds "dysfunctional beliefs regarding relationships" were more prone to divorce than those in which both parties had a more realistic and rational understanding of marriage.

My own experience as a counselor has taught me that many couples who are seriously dating, engaged, or at least contemplating marriage, have already fallen victim to lies that can be destructive and harmful. Let's take a look at some of the most common lies people believe about engagement.

ENGAGEMENT LIES

Now that I'm engaged I'm irrevocably committed. That means I'm doing a bad thing if I think critically about my fiancé or if I continue to evaluate the wisdom of marrying this person.

But the truth is: You are not irrevocably committed until you stand in front of a preacher or justice of the peace and say, "I do." It is not wrong, during your engagement period, to be seriously contemplating the lifelong commitment you're about to make. When we were engaged, my wife Cindy and I frequently prayed, "Lord, if this marriage is not Your will, please make it obvious to both of us. We don't want to make a mistake with lifelong implications." We both entered into marriage completely convinced that we were doing the right thing, and our life together over the last eleven years has shown us that we *were* right.

It's better to marry someone I'm not sure about than to suffer the embarrassment of breaking an engagement.

But the truth is: Embarrassment over a broken engagement may last for several weeks or months, but the payback for entering into marriage with the wrong person can be very long and very painful. It may take the rest of your life to deal with a mistake that large. Many clients have told me, "I knew on the day I got married that it was a mistake."

My question is, "If you knew it was a mistake, why did you go through with it?"

Usually I'll get an answer something like, "What else could I have done? It was too late to back out of it."

The truth is that no matter how hard or embarrassing it will be to break off an engagement, this pain and suffering cannot begin to compare to the years of misery which will follow a marriage between two people who are poorly suited for each other.

Since we're engaged and going to get married anyway, there's no harm in getting involved sexually.

But the truth is: Being engaged does *not* necessarily mean you're going to be getting married. Actually, twenty-five percent of all engagements break up, at least temporarily. So if you are a Christian who values your virginity and your chastity, be careful! Getting sexually involved with someone, even if it's someone you're engaged to, and then seeing the relationship dissolve, can be emotionally and spiritually devastating.

The Bible clearly says that the sexual union is reserved for marriage. Why? Not because God is some cosmic killjoy who wants to keep us from having a good time. When God gives a law, He always does so with the greatest good of His creatures in mind. When He says that sex is not for the "almost-married," but for husbands and wives, He has very good reasons for doing so. Josh McDowell's *Why Wait?* (San Bernardino: Here's Life Publications, 1987.)is an excellent treatise on the benefits of waiting until marriage to get involved sexually and the dangers of not waiting.

While some people make the argument that there is no "formula" for a wedding ceremony found in the Bible, it is obvious that there was a ceremony that publicly and privately sealed the commitment between one man and one woman. After all, Jesus' first recorded miracle took place at a wedding (John 2:1–11), and His parable of the wise and foolish virgins also revolves around a wedding ceremony. Furthermore, there is much in the way of wedding imagery throughout the New Testament, where the relationship between Christ and His church is often described in terms of the relationship between a bride and groom.

We have been having sex and have to marry because the Bible says you shouldn't have sex with anyone other than your spouse. It's better to marry this person I'm unsure of rather than deal with the guilt of having sex with someone I decided not to marry.

But the truth is: God doesn't expect you to perform a lifetime of penance for your sins, and that's what you would be doing by entering into a potentially painful, harmful marriage just because you had been engaging in sexual intercourse with the other person. If this is how you are feeling, you need to remember that every human being on this planet has sinned at one time or another, and the only way any of us can obtain forgiveness for those sins is through the blood of Christ. If you've committed the sin of having sex outside of marriage, confess it, ask for God's forgiveness, and then go on with your life. God isn't going to beat you up everyday for the rest of your life—or constantly remind you that you made a mistake—so why do it to yourself?

And remember, when you sincerely ask God to forgive

you for something you've done, He does it. Then He forgets about it, so you can forget about it, too. Sexual intercourse between two unmarried people is not the unpardonable sin. There's no reason in the world why you should spend the rest of your life paying for such a mistake, but counseling experience has taught me that this is exactly what many well-meaning Christians wind up doing. And I think it's important for me to say that it's not always the woman who feels that she has to marry someone because she's been having sex with him.

I have had men tell me things like, "I had to marry her, because she gave me her virginity." Or, "I ruined her for anyone else." Of course, that latter statement is just oozing and dripping with presumption, even though it may be well-intentioned. But it certainly doesn't make the "sin" of premarital sex any less damaging by moving ahead into a marriage that you both know is going to wind up as a disaster. And there can be real trouble when the husband and wife are looking at each other over the dinner table and each is thinking, "I *had* to marry you because you seduced me."

Please don't compound your problems by marrying the wrong person simply because you've been to bed with him or her.

I know we have had some problems while we were dating, but I'm sure those will fade away once we're married.

But the truth is: If you've been having serious problems now, then you'd better throw this fish back in the ocean, because World War III is liable to break out once you've said, "I do."

See, marriage magnifies everything. Not only will the

problems you've had during your dating period *not* fade away, but they are likely to grow bigger and more troubling. After all, if there is ever a time when two people are willing to overlook each other's faults, that time is when they are dating, falling in love, and deciding to get married.

If you're a woman, you need to know:

- If he's abusive during the courtship, he will be even more abusive once you're married to him
- If he drinks too much now, he will drink too much when you're his wife
- If he flirts with other women now, then you can know *for sure* that he'll flirt after you're married

If you're a man, you should know:

- If she's verbally abusive and sharp-tongued now, you haven't seen anything compared to what she'll be like once you've said your vows
- If she's habitually late for almost everything and that really "bugs" you, it will drive you right up the wall once you're married to her
- If she likes to spend money while you like to hold on to it, don't think marriage will suddenly make you compatible when it comes to the handling of finances

Now, in the statements I've just made, please understand that I'm not trying to single out men and women as being guilty of certain kinds of misbehavior. In other words, it may be the woman who is physically abusive or who drinks to excess, and it may be the man who is habitually late or who throws money around irresponsibly. But over and over and over again I have had people sit in my office, tears running down their cheeks, and tell me, "I really thought I could change him!" Please, please remember that whatever major differences exist between you and your partner will not be dissolved by the wedding ceremony. There are no magical words in the wedding vows, nor is there any power in the rice (or, these days, the birdseed) the wedding guests throw at you.

So if there are problems between you, *now* is the time to deal with them, not after you've already become Mr. and Mrs.

Incidentally, sometimes the qualities that initially attract people become a problem given the day-after-day closeness of the marriage relationship. I know this from experience, because before she married me, Cindy found my naturally extroverted and outgoing behavior to be quite appealing and entertaining (or so she said). But, once we began living together seven days a week, fifty-two weeks a year, she occasionally found the same behavior to be—well—"obnoxious." (Her word.) We've worked on that, though, and I try to tone it down when I see that my sparkling personality is getting to be a bit much for her, and she, meanwhile, does her best to be tolerant of me, even when she doesn't feel much like it.

What pollster Sydney J. Harris says is puzzling but true: "Why is it that when married couples separate, they so often tend to blame each other for the very qualities that attracted them to each other in the first place?"

As long as we love each other, that's all that matters. Everything else will work out.

But the truth is: People don't always understand what love is. As we've discussed previously, they confuse love with romance, and the two are not always even in the same ballpark. Romantic feelings can come and go. They can be very intense in the morning and then all but disappear by the end of the day—or vice versa. Besides, marriage isn't always very romantic. It isn't romantic when the baby has an ear infection and keeps you up all night walking the floor. It isn't romantic when your spouse tells you that your family budget just isn't working out, and the two of you are going to have to sit down and make some major adjustments in your spending habits.

In other words, a marriage takes lots and lots of hard work! Have you ever heard the old hymn that asks, "Must I be carried to the skies on flowery beds of ease?" Well, if you think for a moment that any marriage consists of floating through life on those flowery beds of ease, you need a heavy dose of reality therapy. Life involves conflict, and that means marriage involves conflict. There will be challenges to overcome, disappointments to deal with, messes to clean up, tears to be dried, angry words to be forgiven, and storms to walk through.

I realize that I'm talking an awful lot about the negative aspects of married life, but that's because anyone who's contemplated marriage needs to be reminded that life is not always going to be beautiful sunsets and rainbows. The sunsets and rainbows we all know about already.

Now, a disclaimer about all that I've just said. If, when you're saying, "All we need is love," you're talking about the type of love that's mentioned in the thirteenth chapter of 1 Corinthians, then, okay, you're right.

If it is the type of love that "suffers long and is kind; . . .

does not envy; . . . does not parade itself, is not puffed up; does not behave rudely, does not seek its own, is not provoked, thinks no evil; does not rejoice in iniquity, but rejoices in the truth; bears all things, believes all things, hopes all things, endures all things" (1 Cor. 13:4–7), if it is the type of love that "never fails," then it is, indeed, all you need. After all, that is the same type of love God has toward us—a love that is not based upon our merit or worthiness, but upon His grace, and which flows from His power, and not our own.

Premarital counseling is a waste of time. You are either compatible with someone or you're not, and all the counseling in the world won't really make any difference.

But the truth is: I know this next story sounds kind of strange, but I also know that it really happened. I was counseling a young couple who were just about to be married when the subject of children came up. The woman was surprised to hear her fiancé say that he didn't want any.

She looked at him like she couldn't believe it. "What are you talking about? I've always wanted a boy and a girl."

"No way! I've never wanted children."

Up until that point in their counseling, they were doing fine. They seemed to be very well suited for each other. But they had never talked to each other regarding how they felt about children. They were just moving ahead on the wrong assumption that they both felt the same way.

Not only didn't they feel the same way, but they both held very strong opinions. Unfortunately, they could not reach an understanding on this very crucial issue, and the engagement was broken. But it was far better to find out *before* marriage that they had such major differences of opinion.

It's not often that premarital counseling uncovers such a dramatic difference in attitudes. But it does often reveal those little differences that can turn into big problems later on, and it gives couples a better foundation for dealing with those potentially difficult areas.

Every couple contemplating marriage needs premarital counseling, because it can help make the difference between success and failure in a marriage.

For one thing, premarital counseling has changed significantly during the last ten to fifteen years. The researchers Markman, Floyd, Stanley, and Storaasli identify in their article, "Prevention of Marital Distress: A Longitudinal Investigation" (*Journal of Consulting and Clinical Psychology*, 1988), that counseling is beginning to show significant beneficial effects, both in terms of decreasing the divorce rate, and in terms of maintaining premarital levels of relationship satisfaction.

It's important to remember, too, that initial compatibility in terms of likes, dislikes, temperaments, and personality styles does not ensure a happy or successful marriage. There are deeper issues involved, and premarital counseling can help to uncover and deal with these issues.

Living together will tell us whether or not our marriage will be successful.

But the truth is: Just the opposite. Research has shown that couples who live together before marriage have a significantly higher divorce rate than those who don't live together first. In fact, one study has shown that the risk of getting divorced is approximately one-third greater for those couples who lived together first and then got married.

I know that flies in the face of the world's wisdom, but it is a fact nevertheless. Statistically speaking, living together prior to marriage is *not* beneficial. Entering into a marriage is not the same as buying a car: You don't get a chance to take it on a test drive.

Now that we've discussed eight lies engaged couples sometimes believe, let's talk about some lies that men and women often take with them into marriage.

MARRIAGE MYTHS

Marriage is the key to a fulfilled and happy life.

But the truth is: The key to a fulfilled life is a growing, vibrant relationship with the One who created you. Seeking to gain fulfillment via any other means, including marriage to a loving partner, is futile. Now, I'm *not* knocking marriage. A good marriage can be one of God's greatest gifts to humankind—but it is not the be-all and end-all of human existence.

If you think of marriage as the key to your personal fulfillment, what you're really doing is demanding that your spouse make you happy. As I mentioned before, happiness is an internal affair. It's up to *you* to be happy within yourself. Depending upon any other person to make you happy and fulfilled is unfair, both to you and to that other person. This attitude will eventually lead to resentment on the part of both partners, as in:

"She doesn't make me happy," and, "He depends on me to make him happy all the time, and sometimes it's just too much for me. I want to scream!"

Sure she wants to scream. It is too much of a burden to be charged with the responsibility of bringing happiness and fulfillment into another person's life. True happiness is something only God can give.

If you are unhappy as a single person, you are probably going to be unhappy as a married person. What you must do is come to grips with the real reason for your unhappiness. Unless you reach the point where you really feel comfortable with yourself, when you're happy and contented by yourself, then nobody else is going to be able to "make" you happy.

If you are anxious to get married because you think finding your life's partner will bring fulfillment and happiness into your life, I'm afraid you're headed for a big disappointment.

Happiness is the main purpose of marriage.

But the truth is: The main purpose of marriage is to glorify God, and one way God is best glorified is by two people demonstrating self-sacrificing love and commitment to each other. If you think that God invented marriage as a means of making us happy, then it's easy to walk away from a marriage that doesn't make you happy. It's easy to think, "Well, I'm unhappy being married to this person, and I know God doesn't want me to be unhappy, so I'm going to get a divorce. I'm sure He'll understand." Not true. What God wants is for you to work together to overcome whatever problems might be causing you and your partner to be unhappy with each other.

Remember that no relationship is happy all the time.

My commitment to Christ will guarantee that my marriage will work.

But the truth is: God doesn't force people to respond to each other in a godly manner. In other words, just because you are a Christian doesn't guarantee that your spouse will be one (or act like one), too, and it takes two people to make a marriage work.

If our relationship takes hard work, we must not be right for each other. Good relationships happen spontaneously.

But the truth is: Anything that looks effortless generally takes a great deal of work. For example, watch a couple of figure skaters gliding over the ice during the Winter Olympics, and it looks so easy, so smooth. They move together so gracefully. But what you don't see are the days, weeks, and months of practice that went into perfecting that routine, the long grueling hours spent on the ice in an effort to make everything look so easy.

The same thing is true of romantic relationships. If you know of a marriage that seems to be "made in heaven," I can almost guarantee you that a lot of it was made right here on earth, too, with old-fashioned hard work and perseverance. In fact, I would go so far as to say that *no* marriage will work without a great deal of effort.

Once we marry, we are *all* very hard to live with.

In other words, I don't care how great your future husband seems to be, there are still going to be times when he's grumpy, unreasonable, demanding, and forgetful. He will make mistakes. He'll disappoint you. He may forget your anniversary or your birthday. He may even go out and spend a bunch of money on something—such as a ten-thousand dollar fishing lure that attracts fish via radio waves—or a combination Veg-o-Matic cassette tape player that chops vegetables to a disco beat.

And I don't care how wonderful and sweet your ladylove is, there will still be times when she's feeling depressed and/or angry and when she might take it out on you, even though (naturally) you haven't done a single thing to deserve such treatment.

What should you do when your love acts unfairly and unreasonably toward you? One option to consider is going back and reading the thirteenth chapter of 1 Corinthians for a refresher course on the meaning of love, and then try to live up to that definition.

My spouse can and should meet most, if not all, of my needs.

But the truth is: God has created us in such a way that no one person can meet all or most of our needs. We need a relationship with Him, we need interdependent friendships outside of marriage, we need hobbies, exercise, and so on.

Now some people turn this around and think that they're responsible for meeting all of their spouses' needs. But if you feel that way, you're going to enter marriage with a burden that's impossible to carry. During the wedding vows, you will promise to love, honor, and cherish your mate. You will not promise to meet all of his or her needs. That's just an impossibility.

Besides, even if you threw all of your efforts into satisfying your partner, chances are good that over time the other person's needs would become larger and more demanding. That's just the way human nature works. When you give and give and give to people, they generally become more and more willing to take, and less and less satisfied by your efforts.

If my partner and I don't always feel love for each other, that means our relationship is in trouble.

But the truth is: Love is more than a feeling. Yes, those "warm and fuzzy" feelings of romance are wonderful, but they may come and go. The deeper aspects of true love transcend feelings and have more to do with commitment than emotion.

If I want it to be pleasing to Christ, then I should think only of my partner's needs. I want this relationship to be all it can be. Worrying about what I want or desire is selfish and sinful.

But the truth is: That type of thinking is wrong on two counts. First, because worrying only about your partner's needs and desires isn't fair to him or her. It allows him to become selfish and self-indulgent and, in the long-term, it may prevent him from knowing the joy of doing everything within his power to meet your needs. And it *is* a joy to try to meet the needs of someone you love.

Second of all, God created us so that we have certain needs which must be met in order for us to function to our fullest capabilities. When our individual needs are not met, we suffer, and we are less able to help meet the needs of others. When He walked this earth in the flesh, Jesus Christ took time out to see that His own needs were met. Often, He went off into a secluded place to pray to be away from the crowds who always demanded so much of his time, energy, and attention. Sometimes, He went off with three of His closest disciples—Peter, James, and John, because

He needed some closer, more intimate relationships than were possible to have with twelve men all at once.

You are a human being. You're not a superhero who can go through life giving and giving and never worrying about yourself. Do that, and others (your partner included) may suck the very life out of you. You will be a victim of burnout, and if your relationship doesn't fail completely, it will at least become a source of aggravation and oppression.

WHAT LIES HAVE YOU BELIEVED?

Can you now see where you have had erroneous ideas about engagement and marriage (if, indeed, you *have* believed some of the lies we've discussed)?

The problem is that some of these lies may be so deeply ingrained into your thinking that it's hard to discard them. How can you do that? How can you combat the hold some of these lies may have on your intellect and your emotions?

The first thing you have to do is recognize them for what they are: lies.

In order to overcome belief in lies, we have to know what lies we believe, and what it is that has made us come to believe them. You can't fight a lie if you don't know it's there—and sometimes it's easier to accept a lie than to believe the truth.

Next up, a look at a very important issue in any male-female relationship. That issues is: Communication. We'll talk specifically about some more lies people believe regarding this important aspect of a relationship, and we'll give some concrete ways you can reject those lies in favor of the truth.

Four

But You Didn't Hear It the Way I Meant It

W hen the late George Romney was seeking the Republican nomination for President back in 1964, he said something like this:

"I know you think you heard what I meant to say, but what you heard wasn't really what I said."

Or something similar.

The Michigan governor's statement, as difficult as it may have been to understand, really had one central thought, and that is, "Boy, communicating can be difficult sometimes!"

That's for sure!

Learning how to communicate properly is vitally important in any relationship, but especially in a love relationship between a man and a woman.

In recent years there have been literally dozens of books written on the different ways men and women hear and say things. One of the most recent of those books proclaims that "Men Are from Mars, Women Are from Venus" (New York: Harper Collins, 1992.)

Well . . . that's one way to put it. After all, we have so much difficulty communicating between different cultures here on earth, one can just imagine how very difficult it would be to open lines of dialogue between creatures that came from different planets.

Miscommunication is one of the leading reasons why relationships fail. People don't know how to say things properly, or they don't know how to listen attentively. They don't know when to speak up and when not to speak up, and they expect too much out of their partners with regard to interpreting nonverbal clues and reading minds. There are bound to be times in any relationship where communication goes awry: You're saying one thing and your partner is hearing something else, and vice versa. You can be like Abbott and Costello trying to back the car out of the driveway. While Costello is driving, Abbott says, "Back up . . ." and then adds, "Go ahead." Costello starts to back up, but then when his partner says "go ahead," he becomes confused and stops.

"What do you want me to do?" he asks.

"Go ahead," Abbott replies. "Back up."

Of course, Costello is exasperated because he has started to pull forward, but then his friend has told him to "back up."

Well, of course, those two could take a simple routine

like that and keep it going for many minutes. But a lot of people play those kinds of games in their romantic relationships. They don't want to be running around in circles, not knowing when to back up and when to go ahead, or even who's on first, but they just can't communicate properly!

There is help, though. Knowing some of the common ways people misunderstand each other can help you reduce the number of times when you and your partner might as well be speaking different languages. There are certain lies about communication that can help you, if you know what they are and why they're wrong.

Partners must be totally open and honest with each other all the time.

But the truth is: Honesty without love, tact, and diplomacy can be painful and harmful to a relationship. There are simply some times when the full expression of your emotions and thoughts is inappropriate and best reserved for later.

For example:

"Honey, do you think that girl is pretty?"

"Pretty! I think she's gorgeous! Stunning! Hubba hubba! Va-va-voom!!"

Well, he might be telling the absolute, total truth in a situation like that—but it's not very smart of him, and he'd better hope he likes dog biscuits, because he'll probably be sleeping with Rover tonight. (And he'll need to bring along an ice pack to help take care of those bumps on his head.)

Or suppose he has just bought the most hideous jacket

anyone has ever seen . . . but for some reason he's proud of it.

"Well, dear, what do you think?"

"I think you look like Bozo the Clown's brother . . . that's what I think."

Okay, I realize that these are pretty dramatic examples, and that most of us would have a bit more tact than to say such things to someone we really care about. But these are overly blatant examples of things supposedly loving couples say to each other all the time.

Even if you feel a need to criticize your loved one, pick your time and place wisely, and do it as gently and lovingly as possible. And even though some may think this doesn't sound very "Christian" of me, I believe there are times when the truth doesn't need to be spoken. For example, even if a man does think another woman is absolutely beautiful, there's nothing at all wrong with his saying, "Do I think *she's* pretty? Oh, honey, you know I think you're the most beautiful woman in the world." If a man says something like that, his partner may say, "Oh, come on. Quit flattering me!" But you know what? She may protest, but she's going to like it just the same.

Another area where "total honesty" is not recommended is in sharing the details of past romantic encounters. There is no need to give out all the details of previous relationships in the guise of being honest. Telling all the details about whom you dated, how you felt about them, how far your relationship went and so on can be harmful because it can lead to jealousy and insecurity. You would have to be a pretty secure person to hear details such as these and not experience negative emotions.

There is especially no need to share all of the sexual

details with one another. I would hope that any Christian couple would save sex until after marriage, and I would hope that both the man and woman would be virgins on their wedding day. But because I live in the real world, I know this isn't always, or even most often, the case.

I don't think there's any need at all to discuss past sexual encounters, even if it's just to tell your present partner how much "better" he or she is than your previous partner(s). Your intentions may be good, but they can be damaging. I've seen many examples of couples putting distance between themselves by such "honesty," and it can be very hard to undo the damage, like trying to get toothpaste back in the tube once it's all been squeezed out.

Playwright Bernard Slade has come up with a number of excellent lines for his play *Special Occasions* (New York: Samuel French, 1982), but one of the best is when the man asks his ex-wife why she has just told him something that she knew would hurt him so much. "At least," she replies, "when I hurt you I know what I'm doing." The implication, of course, is that he has said and done many things to hurt her, without even realizing what he was doing.

It's always important to put yourself in your partner's place. The Golden Rule applies to communication, too. How would you like to have someone say to you what you are about to say to the one you love? If it would hurt you, then chances are very good that it would hurt your loved one, too . . . so check your style and motivation before speaking.

If my partner really loves me, he (or she) will know and understand my needs and wants without me telling him directly.

But the truth is: If your partner could read your mind, he'd be making his living by appearing on TV talk shows, where he'd amaze members of the audience by reading their minds, and he'd have a name like "The Amazing Kreskin."

And, quite honestly, I don't much believe in mind reading anyway!

Expecting your love to read your mind can get you into a lot of trouble.

The stereotypical picture of this is the man coming home from work to find his mate sitting on the sofa, head in hands, crying her eyes out.

"Why, honey, what's wrong?"

"Well, if you don't know, I'm sure not going to tell you."

But it is not women alone who expect their partners to be mind readers. Men are every bit as good at playing this game, and maybe even better.

For example, earlier I mentioned The Amazing Kreskin. He's been thrilling audiences for years with his mind-reading tricks. But you know what? He's been married several times. So apparently he wasn't so amazing when it came to reading his wives' minds and knowing what they needed to keep them happy!

Anyway, it's unfair to expect your partner to read your mind. If you've been dropping hint after hint about something you need or want and he just doesn't understand you, I'll admit that he's not being very sensitive. But love means that you be willing to overlook that insensitivity and express yourself clearly and in as straightforward a manner as possible instead of becoming angry and pouting.

Remember that different nonverbal behaviors can mean totally different things in different circumstances. For example, in some cases a person who has his arms crossed over his chest can be indicating that he is feeling defensive. But then again, it might just be that he's cold and wants you to turn up the heat.

Another thing to keep in mind is that people are imperfect, and because of this they may sometimes forget what we have told them, even with regard to our wants and needs. Just because someone may have forgotten something you told him doesn't mean he doesn't love you. It just means he's human and, like all humans, prone to forgetfulness.

Positive feedback is not as important to a relationship as direct and honest communication about our complaints and concerns.

But the truth is: If you love someone you will just naturally enjoy giving him or her positive feedback. You will delight in telling them how good they look, what a good job they've done, how much you enjoy being with them, how much you appreciate the things they do for you, and so on.

Research by George Rekers and his associates, reported in *Family Building: Six Qualities of a Strong Family* (Ventura, CA: Regal Books, 1985), has shown that a tendency to appreciate one another, and to express that appreciation, is one of the distinguishing makers of a healthy family. We all need positive feedback, especially from people we care about, and you can chalk that one up, once again, to the fact that we are all "only human."

If you've ever watched an animal trainer at work, you know that positive reinforcement plays an important role: A dog sits up on command and he's rewarded with a treat . . . a dolphin does a back flip and she gets a couple of yummy mackerel. Now please don't think for a minute that I'm equating men and women with dogs and dolphins. But even on the level of animals, positive reinforcement is important, and it's still important when it comes to higher animals—like us.

Actually, it is the decrease of positive behaviors between lovers that is often responsible for the gradual decrease in their satisfaction with their relationships. Another thing to keep in mind is that whereas positive feedback increases the likelihood that desirable behaviors will continue, a lack of positive feedback increases the likelihood that desirable behaviors will stop. In other words, if I don't thank my partner for doing something kind for me, chances are that she won't want to do the same thing again. And who could blame her?

Actor Walter Matthau has been quoted as saying in *From "I Do" to "I'll Sue"*, "My first wife never complimented me on the way I looked, but Carol says I am the handsomest man in the world. Believe it or not, that made a big change in my life" (New York: Plume/Meridian, 1993). Matthau's first marriage ended in divorce after ten years. Surely, he doesn't really think he's the handsomest man in the world, but he knows that's how his wife sees him, and he's been happily married to her for thirty-five years!

In any argument, one person is always right and the other person is always wrong. The goal of an argument is to prove that you are the one who is right, to attain a position where you can say, "See! I told you I was right!

But the truth is: Your partner should never be thought of as your opponent. The two of you are on the same team. If you view your relationship as a competition, or if you're always trying to prove that you're right while your partner is wrong, then yours is not likely to be a story with an ending of "and they lived happily ever after."

Please remember that you and your partner have a common opponent, and that is Satan—along with the outside forces he will use to tear at your partnership. The truth is that in any argument that comes about between two well-meaning people there are probably degrees of right and wrong on both sides. Often, the argument results from looking at the same issue from two very different perspectives, and both of you would be wise to look for common ground. It doesn't take a whole lot of effort to say, "You know, I can see your point about that, and I understand how you feel, but let me try to explain how I see it." Using statements like that can help to defuse the situation before it escalates out of control. It can also help to show your romantic interest that the most important thing to you is getting the issue resolved, and *not* proving who's right or wrong.

An acquaintance of mine is a journalism teacher who constantly reminds his first-year college students of the importance of being observant. At some point during the year, he tests them in what I think is an interesting way. Specifically, he will have someone his students haven't seen before interrupt the class for some reason or another.

Perhaps it will be a student who will wander in during the middle of class and ask loudly where he can find the photo lab. Or it might be a woman who says she's looking for the registrar's office. It doesn't have to be a big deal . . . just enough of a deal to disrupt the class. Then, after the person leaves, he asks his students to get out pen and paper and describe what just happened. How old was the person? What was his hair color? What was he wearing?

You'd be amazed at how people have changed in a matter of minutes! Some of them have aged rapidly, or dropped years in an instant. People who were wearing suits have been described as wearing blue jeans or shorts, tank tops have turned to floor-length dresses, hair color has changed from blonde to black, mustaches show up on people who had none before, and beards and eyeglasses disappear. In some instances people have even changed sex.

Well, this shows that freshman journalism students aren't always the most observant people in the world. It also shows that it's easy for people not to see things the same way. It's natural for there to be differences of opinion and conflicting ideas. People are prone to hearing things differently, seeing things differently, and describing them differently.

Usually, my friend will find that most of the descriptions have one or two elements of truth. Occasionally, even the most unobservant student will pick up on one or two particularly important truths that nobody else noticed.

What am I saying? That it is human nature to see things differently, so don't expect your partner to see everything the way you do. Cut him some slack, and, like I said before, always remember that you two are on the same team!

In a happy relationship there will be very few, if any, disagreements or conflicts.

But the truth is: Every intimate relationship will have a significant number of conflicts and disagreements.

The only relationships that are without conflict are

superficial. For example, I've never had an argument with my mailman, even though he's someone I see on a regular basis. I just don't know him well enough, nor does he know me well enough, for us to start a fight with each other.

It's not really avoiding conflicts that's important, but rather how conflicts are handled when they come along. It is possible to "argue" in a respectful, loving way—and to ask for and give forgiveness on those occasions when a conflict may get a little bit too heated (as it occasionally will, human nature being what it is).

Conflict isn't always bad. It can be a growth process. It can be one of the ways you and your partner get to know each other better. It can be the means by which you learn the art of compromise and collaboration. When conflict is addressed in an assertive, healthy, and loving fashion, it can actually *increase* intimacy and satisfaction. On the other hand, avoiding conflict can be unhealthy. It is the stuffing of anger down inside of you rather than getting it out in the open and dealing with it that can cause bitterness and decreased intimacy. The Bible describes this process as allowing a "root of bitterness" to grow inside of you (Heb. 12:15), and a root of bitterness can eventually strangle any relationship.

So you see, how well and how effectively a couple "fights" can play a huge role in how happy and stable their relationship will be.

Romantic partners should see eye to eye on every issue and work toward having identical viewpoints.

But the truth is: I know of a couple whose marriage has lasted for more than forty years. This husband and wife have done an excellent job of rearing four children, and it's obvious to everyone who knows them that they still enjoy being together, even after all these years. But you know what? He's a life-long Democrat. She's a life-long Republican.

Only once or twice in all the years they've been together have they voted for the same presidential candidate. What's more, they usually don't agree on state or local elections either. She'll never be able to understand how he can vote for so many "tax-and-spend" liberals, and he can't figure for the life of him how his sweet, loving wife could cast her vote for so many "mean-spirited right-wingers."

Now conventional wisdom says that the very best way to get involved in a conflict is to start talking about politics or religion, and I would not be in a hurry to recommend a marriage between two people who have such diametrically opposed political viewpoints. But in this instance, it works. It works because these people truly love each other, despite their differences, and they've learned to live with them. They know they're never going to change each other, but they respect and love each other enough so that they don't feel that they *have* to change each other.

You see, disagreement on some issues—even important ones like politics—does not necessarily have to stand in the way of romantic happiness. Two other things to keep in mind:

1. While general agreement on many of the major aspects of life together is important, differences in background, experiences, and personality type make this impossible to achieve on all fronts.
2. Total agreement on everything is boring. When used constructively, different outlooks can provide a

couple with more options when solving problems, working on projects, and so on.

I love to go to Baskin-Robbins 31 Flavors for ice cream. Sometimes I'll even try a really "weird" flavor like watermelon or bubblegum. I may not be crazy about the new flavor, but it's still fun to try it. And you know, it would be kind of boring if it was "Baskin-Robbins One Flavor." If all they had was vanilla, or chocolate, I doubt if they'd be doing such a booming business.

Diversity can be a *great thing!*

Coming up next, I'm going to show you what a healthy relationship looks like. Stay tuned!

Five

A Blueprint for a Healthy Relationship

What does a healthy marriage look like? Can we get a good idea from watching old television shows from the 1950s and 1960s? Is it like *Father Knows Best*, where Jim Anderson always knows exactly what to say in every situation? Or how about *Leave it to Beaver*, where Ward and June always relate to each other with grace and humor, and somehow manage to survive all of the hilarious hijinks of Wally and the Beaver.

Well, unfortunately, that's television, and this is real life. In television, whatever problems may come up are usually neatly resolved within the next thirty minutes—or sixty, at the most. In mythical television cities, like Springfield and Mayfield, the sun is always shining, nobody's ever sick, and there are no financial pressures. What's more, nobody ever loses a job, or is threatened with losing one, and the major issues are usually something as simple as whether Princess should break her date with the boy who asked her to the prom first, since the boy she really wanted to go with all along has now asked her. In a world like this, even the villain—a guy like Eddie Haskell—is relatively harmless.

Ah, wouldn't it be great if real life were like that? But we all know it isn't. In real life there are problems that are not easily resolved. Life is messy, lumpy, and there are some issues that may never be resolved to our complete satisfaction. There are problems, pressures, challenges, and obstacles to be overcome.

Yes, it's easy to have a perfect family, a perfect marriage, and a perfect relationship on TV where everything is neatly scripted. It's not so easy to have one out here in the real world!

Believe me, as a clinical psychologist I know how hard it can be. I spend almost every day talking to people who are struggling to make their relationships work. In more than thirteen years of counseling people I have never had someone tell me:

"Dr. Nicholson, I just wanted to come in so I could tell you how well my life has been going. I've always had wonderful relationships with both of my parents and all my brothers and sisters. I have a number of close and supportive friends, but my spouse is my very best friend of all. He is so supportive and wonderful when it comes to meeting all my needs. What's more, my children are a delight and my daily walk with the Lord is a constant source of strength, joy, and inspiration. Well, I guess that's all I really wanted to say. Here's your fee. Hope you have a nice day."

If anyone ever does sit in my office and tell me something like that, I'm going to start looking around for Rod Serling or Alan Funt, because I'll know that *I'm* on television.

Instead of talking to people who are deliriously happy and contented, I spend most of my time talking to those who are interested in improving less-than-satisfactory situations.

And yet, it is important that we take the time to look at relationships that are working well. The importance of having healthy role models is something the world of psychology is coming to understand and appreciate. We are beginning to see that we can learn a great deal about relationships by studying people who are functioning in healthy ways. This makes sense, doesn't it? Would you study the style of a strikeout king to learn the art of hitting . . . or turn to Charlie Brown to learn how to kick a field goal? Of course not. Most often you can learn more by studying success than by analyzing failure.

In this chapter, I want to summarize some of the most recent findings of some experimental and clinical studies of strong relationships.

Just take a look at the statistics related to marriage, and you'll see that marital bliss is hard to come by: Nearly half of all marriages end in divorce. Approximately 63 percent of all children will live in a single-parent household for at least some time prior to their eighteenth birthday. From statistics like these, it's easy to see that many, if not most, American youths and singles have never been exposed to a healthy role model of what a marriage needs to be—at least not on a regular day-in and day-out basis. Because you're interested in marriage (or because someone you know is interested in marriage for you and gave you this book), let's take a look at some of the ingredients of a healthy relationship.

Start with Two Healthy Adults

Perhaps it's obvious, but in order for a relationship to be healthy, the people who are involved in that relationship must be healthy. What about you? How emotionally healthy are you? These next items may give you some insight.

- How much do you depend upon your parents?
- Are you capable of functioning on your own? (Can you manage your own financial affairs, take care of your own housing, food, and transportation needs? I know it sounds silly, but I have actually come across married couples who didn't even know how to do their own laundry.)
- Do you know what you want in life? Do you have specific goals and do you have a realistic plan to work toward those goals?
- Are you basically happy with who you are? Do you like yourself?
- Do you understand that your happiness is not dependent upon the person you love, but that his or her presence in your life will add a richness to your existence?

If you see that you are still quite dependent upon your

parents, if you're not sure how to function on your own, don't know for sure what you want in life, don't really feel good about yourself, and think your life depends on your partner being a part of it . . . then it is not the best time for you to be thinking about marriage. You have some growing up and some healing to do.

And once you've taken an honest as possible look at yourself, try to make an honest assessment of how your partner shapes up in all of these areas.

I have had unhappy wives tell me, "I didn't realize how much of an influence his mother still had on him." And I've had husbands tell me things like, "She can't go more than a day or two without talking to her mother, and when anything important comes up, she's on the phone asking Mom what to do." That is unhealthy. Anyone who is contemplating marriage needs to be free from his or her parents' control. That doesn't mean that you shouldn't have a good, loving relationship with your parents, or that you won't respect them and weigh their advice carefully when they give it. But in a healthy marriage, both partners give their allegiance to their spouse, and not to Mom and Dad.

Here's another frequent complaint: "I knew before I married him that he'd had a number of jobs, but I figured that he was just trying to find himself . . . that eventually he'd find something he liked and he'd stick with it. But it just hasn't happened. He bounces around from job to job, and he always finds some reason to quit. I just don't think I can take it anymore."

Hey, lady, let me tell you something. If the guy's had seventeen different jobs in three years, chances are that it's *not* because he's versatile. You see, if a man or woman is unstable in his or her personal life, he or she will bring that instability into the marriage, and you can bet that there will be problems.

For a relationship to work, both partners must have a healthy view of who they are and what they want out of life. And, as much as they love and depend upon each other, both partners must know that if it became necessary they would be able to function without the other. The healthy person does not believe things like, "I couldn't live without you," or, "If I lost you, I'd just die," or, "You are my reason for living." Thinking that way is putting too much responsibility on the other person, and the truth is that nobody is responsible for your happiness but you.

Another mark of a healthy person is that he is *mostly* aware of his own opinions, emotions, needs, and desires. He takes responsibility for who he is and doesn't blame anyone else for what he does or says. In other words, he understands that, "I think, feel, and act the way I do because I choose to, and not because anyone else makes me think something, feel something, or do something." Now, you may wonder about my use of the word "mostly." The reason I use that word (and other qualifiers) is that there are times in every human being's life when we are not totally aware of our motivations for doing or feeling certain ways. And I don't want anyone reading this to think that he or she has to be some type of psychological super-human before it's even right to think about getting married. I'm giving high standards to aim for, and I don't expect any human being to hit the mark all of the time.

For example, in all of us, there will be some aspect of personality that keeps us from enjoying life to the fullest. In other words, all of us have some "quirk" that holds us back in some area of life. It might be a neurotic insecurity, an unhealthy behavior or thought pattern, or some other type of peccadillo. The important thing is that we strive to be aware of these problem areas of our personalities and "shrink" them so they become less and less of a difficulty.

The person who has some major areas of weakness, but who isn't the least bit aware of their existence—that's the person who is truly unhealthy. The person who has the same areas of weakness, but who is aware of them and striving to correct them, is usually going to be a more satisfying partner.

Let's move on now to the next ingredient of a healthy relationship.

Putting "We" Ahead of "Me"

In a healthy relationship, both partners put their needs as a couple ahead of their needs as individuals. They also put their relationship with each other ahead of their relationships with others, including their parents or their children. (The one exception to this rule is that your relationship with God needs to be your highest priority in life.)

That doesn't mean that you should consider yourself to be incomplete without the other person, but it does mean that you need to be willing to sacrifice for the good of your mate. Always remember, the strength of the individual increases, rather than weakens, the strength and unity of the couple. This is not a relationship based on neediness or emotional coercion, but on healthy love and respect for each other. You shouldn't always have to worry about proving your strength, but instead be willing to sacrifice, on occasion, for the good of "the team."

Take a lesson from major league baseball. A few years ago the rules of that game changed so that it was easier for players to become free agents, and therefore, to sign new contracts with any team that wanted them. Some teams went on a spending spree like you wouldn't believe. They opened up their big, fat wallets and started throwing money around like it was confetti. They wanted to sign as many of the big stars as they could, and they were willing to spend whatever it took to get them.

But you know what? In most cases, it didn't work out so well. Some of those teams wound up with an amazing array of athletes—but athletes who seemed to be more concerned about their individual statistics than they were about the good of the team. There wasn't that necessary cohesiveness and chemistry that makes for teamwork. There wasn't the willingness to work together, and those "great" teams that looked as if they'd steamroll over the opposition just never got going.

At season's end, some of the teams with the biggest payrolls can usually be found near the bottom of the standings, while the teams that don't have the superstars, but that know what it means to work together, are at or near the top. No, this hasn't happened every time, but it's happened often enough that many teams have decided that they'll stay out of the free-agent bidding wars from now on and go with the homegrown talent.

Now I'm sure you probably know, as I do, some couples who don't seem to spend any time at all together. He's always off with the boys on hunting trips, fishing trips, at the football game—and she's on shopping trips with the girls, or attending a play with her friends. (Or, in today's society, maybe I've got it backward. Maybe *he's* the one on the shopping trips and she's the one hunting and fishing.) At any rate, you have to wonder why two people who act like that ever got married in the first place. Two people who truly love each other will just naturally want to spend time together. Even if it weren't so much common interests that brought them together, they should be wanting to share their lives with each other, each of them learning to enjoy what their partner enjoys.

Of course, in some relationships it's exactly the opposite. The husband and wife rarely spend any time at all away from each other. That's not healthy either, because both partners need some "breathing room," some time to be alone and some time to be with individual friends.

The healthiest couples are those who think of themselves first and foremost as a unit, but who understand the importance of additional outside interests and friendships. This attitude of nurturing the relationship, of always putting "us" first, allows the partnership to flourish and evolve.

When a couple truly values their relationship above everything else in life, they will demonstrate this on a daily basis. They will look for ways to do things for each other, and not with the idea that, "I'm going to do this for you so you'll appreciate me." Remember what we said earlier: A romance is not a competition. I have heard of couples who honestly couldn't seem to do enough for each other, but every little deed was stored up in some kind of imaginary bank account.

"I cooked a wonderful dinner for you today, so now I'm one up on you."

"I sent you flowers, so I guess you owe me one, now."

"I bought you six gifts for your birthday, and you'd better remember that when my birthday comes around."

They didn't talk to each other like that, of course. But their attitudes showed that that was how they felt. It's really important to remember that giving, if it's done with the wrong motives, can be a very selfish thing. To do for each other out of love, out of wanting to please your partner and to demonstrate your love by your actions—that's wonderful. But to do something because you're trying to accumulate "martyr points" is unhealthy and counterproductive.

It might be a difficult question to answer, I realize, but it's a good idea to step back and take a self-inventory at times. Ask yourself, "Am I doing this because I love pleasing my partner, or because *I* want to be noticed and appreciated?" There are times, I'm sure, when all of us would have to admit that our motives come under the latter category. That's human nature. But human nature can be overcome by love.

As you prepare for marriage, remember that the primacy of the marriage relationship means that children, parents, and in-laws are all placed in their proper perspective. Relationships with such people are important, but not nearly as important as the relationship between the man and woman who have chosen to commit their lives to each other.

The Bible says that God's design for marriage is for a man and woman to leave their parents and to "cleave" to each other. You can't cleave to your husband if you're putting your relationship with your mother or father ahead of your relationship with him. You can't cleave to your wife if your relationship with your best fishing buddies takes precedence over your relationship with her.

Another key to a healthy relationship is your ability to communicate with each other.

EFFECTIVE TALKING AND LISTENING

Effective talking and listening is, in other words, communication. I know that doesn't surprise you. Everyone knows that it's important to keep the lines of communication open. It's just that many people don't know how to do it, or, while they may have the "head knowledge" of how to communicate, they don't have the courage to follow through.

Primarily, what I'm talking about is being honest and open with regard to needs, desires, expectations, and opinions—being willing to share what you're thinking instead of stuffing it down and pretending that something doesn't bother you when it does. I'm talking about expressing what's on your mind as clearly and lovingly as possible rather than playing games with each other and thinking, "If you really loved me, you'd know how I feel."

Time now for another quick self-quiz.

You and your partner are going out to dinner, and he suggests a seafood restaurant. The truth is, seafood is the last thing you feel like having tonight. Do you:

A. Go along anyway, not say anything about how you feel, and make do with a small garden salad
B. Blow your gasket and ask why he's always the one who gets to pick where you eat

C. Explain as lovingly as possible that you really just don't feel like seafood tonight, and ask if you can't think of another place that you *and* your partner would both enjoy just as much

Of course, the correct answer would be *C*. If you picked *A*, you might wind up resenting your partner's "selfishness" in taking you to a seafood restaurant, even though, of course, he's not being selfish at all because he doesn't know you don't want seafood tonight. And if you try *B*, your partner is going to resent your attitude. But *C* is the wise choice because you are expressing clearly how you feel, and you're inviting him to do the loving thing by treating you to a dinner that you will both enjoy.

I realize that you might be asking, "What's the big deal about a seafood dinner?" Yes, I know it sounds rather trivial. But unless you can communicate clearly and honestly regarding such small matters, you're probably not going to be able to communicate with each other about the larger things that really are important. And besides, it is not always the big things that destroy a relationship. It's just as likely to be an accumulation of the little things, until that one final straw collapses the wedding plans.

In a healthy relationship, both partners communicate in a way that is so direct and authentic it provides a built-in mechanism for conflict resolution. It is okay to say, "I really don't understand . . ." or "I don't agree with what you're saying because . . ."

Conflicts are not allowed to stay buried below the surface where they can become infected and fester.

At the same time, healthy couples do more than bring their conflicts out into the open. They deal with them! And they do it by working together as respectfully and as lovingly as possible. Thus, unresolved conflicts are not allowed to accumulate and the couple is able to solve problems in a crisis.

I heard a story the other day about a couple of men who were talking about their wives. One of them said, "Whenever we get into an argument, my wife gets historical."

"Don't you mean, *hysterical?*" the other man asked.

"No . . . I mean *historical*. She brings up everything else I've ever done that made her mad."

Well, that's the way some couples communicate. They don't resolve conflicts. They either try to avoid them or bury them, but they never really resolve the issues that caused the conflicts in the first place. Then, whenever another conflict comes along, all of those old unresolved hurts and wounds get dredged back up, and soon irreparable damage is done to the relationship.

I sometimes think of it in terms of a dam on a great river or lake. Whenever there's been a period of too much rain, the water behind the dam can build up to dangerous levels. Engineers have to deal with that by opening some of the floodgates to let the excess water run off. If they don't the weight of the water pressing against the dam will be too much for it to hold, the dam will collapse, and the nearby communities will be swept away by the floodwater.

For a romantic relationship to be all that it ought to be, you have to deal with conflicts and disagreements as they arise. If you allow them to build up, or try to pretend that they don't exist and hide them behind some emotional walls you've built, then sooner or later those walls will come crashing down, and the relationship may be swept away in the ensuing flood.

Don't make the mistake of thinking that "good communication" is always happy communication. There is more to a relationship than love-talk and encouragement. Although, certainly, those things are very important. Good communication means that both partners feel free to express a wide variety of emotions. Not only can we do "happy talk" by expressing love, nurturing, and affirmation through words and touch, but by expressing emotions that less confident couples tend to squelch (such as anger, hurt, confusion, disappointment, etc.). What you're saying is that "I love you so much that it's important for me that you know how I feel about things. And I love you so much that it's important for me to know how *you* feel about things, too."

I've heard it said, and I believe it, that one of the best things you can find in life is someone who knows exactly who you are but who loves you anyway. What I mean by that is that we are all unreasonable at times. We all get our feelings hurt. We all get the blues. We get jealous, even if we know we're being childish. We're human beings, not plaster saints, and we need to feel free to express our human emotions, especially to someone we love enough to marry. And, if you truly love someone, it should be important to you to know how that person is feeling about things. It is the amazing breadth of human experience—laughter, sadness, hurt, embarrassment, fear, joy, and all of the other emotions—that makes human life so diverse and rich.

The truly healthy and happy relationship is one where both partners are able and willing to express their thoughts, feelings, and emotions openly, and allow their partners to do the same.

WHO'S THE BOSS?

Another hallmark of a healthy relationship is that there is no "boss." Both the man and the woman realize that they are partners in all of life, and that theirs is not a superior/subordinate relationship. Neither partner is "in charge" here. Nobody is allowed to make "all the big decisions" by himself or herself.

In a word, what I'm talking about is equality. You've heard the old saying that woman wasn't taken from man's head that she should rule over him, or from his feet that she should serve him, but rather from his side, that she would be his equal and his partner. I like that. There's a lot of truth to it.

In every romantic relationship, there will be some areas where the woman is the stronger, and other areas where the man is the stronger of the two. In the ideal situation, both partners will recognize and be willing to benefit from the strength of the other.

Historically, human society has been dominated by the male, so this is a problem primarily for men, who seem to have trouble relinquishing control to a woman in any area. (It's okay for me to say this. I have the right, being a man myself.) But at the same time, I want to make it clear that I'm not talking about *all* men. Many members of my sex are ready and willing to let their loved ones shine—to see them take positions of leadership in areas where they are the strongest. But we're not all so enlightened.

For example, I know some men who insist on running all the financial affairs of their families, even though they're just not well suited for it. They keep the checkbook, make all the decisions for the family budget, and sometimes even manage to keep their wives in the dark about their family's true financial condition.

Some of these guys have wives who are whizzes when it comes to handling money. They can stretch a dollar farther than the federal government. But their husbands won't take advantage of their wives' strength. They think it's a "manly" thing to be in charge of that area of family life. But that's not true. The "manly" thing would be to know and respect your wife's strengths and allow her to be "in charge" of those areas where she is strongest.

And the opposite is true, too. The woman needs to have a realistic understanding of her strengths as opposed to those of her man, and try not to upstage him or outdo him in areas where he's clearly able to do the best job. In other words, if your boyfriend can whip up dishes that make Julia Child look like a short-order cook and you have trouble boiling water, then by all means, get out of the kitchen and let him cook!

I don't want to overstate the importance of treating each other as equals. I know it seems obvious that this should be the case. But the reality is that in far too many marriages, even Christian marriages, the husband thinks he has the right to be the boss, to tell his wife what to do, how high to jump, and expect her to do it. Because the Bible says that the husband is to be "the head of the wife, as also Christ is the head of the church" (Eph. 5:23), some men think that gives them the authority to do or say anything they feel like, and that their wives can either like it or lump it.

That's hardly fair. It's hardly Christian. It's hardly a proper understanding of the Word of God.

Yes, the Bible does say that the husband is to be the head

of his wife, even as Christ is the head of the church, but then it commands husbands to love their wives as much as Christ loved the church. And how much was that? He loved her so much He was willing to die for her—in fact, He *did* die for her. He doesn't push the church around. He doesn't insult her and make unreasonable demands on her. Instead, He loves and cherishes her so much that He is even willing to suffer and die for her.

Many times, if you look for it, you will find that there is a complementary "fit" between a partner's skills and interests, and thus it is quite natural for leadership areas to fall along complementary lines. For example, if the man is mechanically minded and enjoys tinkering with cars, then he definitely should be the one who takes care of keeping the family vehicles in good running order. In other areas, where the interests and strengths seem to be about equal, the leadership can be handled in shifts. For example, you might plan to take turns paying the bills and handling the family's finances, trading off every year or every few months.

Now some people will insist that the husband and wife should equally divide all of the household duties. Everything they do should be divided right down the middle. Well, it may not work that way, because that may not be the way their skills line up. Hopefully, each is able to exert his or her leadership where natural interests and skills coincide.

For example, in my marriage, I have always been in charge of refuse removal (taking out the trash), outdoor waste relocation (which means that I'm in charge of the pooper-scooper), and handling nutritional provisions for all the subhuman species in our household (feeding the dogs). My wife, Cindy, feels good about my leadership in all of these important and difficult areas and I, in turn, am proud of the job I perform. I know where my skills lie and I use them!

Another hallmark of healthy couples is the ability to look at their relationship realistically.

REALISTIC EXPECTATIONS

Healthy couples think realistically about what their life together will be like. They understand and accept that life can be hard, and that there will be obstacles to overcome and difficulties to face.

When times get tough, healthy couples don't start bemoaning their fates or thinking that God is punishing them for their sins. They understand and accept that life on this fallen planet is far from perfect, and that hard times come to all of us in one way or another.

I'm sure you've heard it said that people react one of two ways when difficulties come to them. They either let their struggles make them "better" or "bitter." In the same way, a couple can work together to overcome whatever challenges they have to face, or they can let those challenges tear them apart, blaming each other because life isn't always tied up in a neat little package like a Walt Disney movie.

Just about any couple can make it gracefully through the good times. They can smile and hold hands and love each other deeply when everyone's healthy, there's plenty of money, and life is grand. But it takes a special relationship to keep on holding each other's hands, to keep on loving each other, when catastrophic illness strikes—as it sometimes will; or when one partner loses his or her job and can't find another one; or when a child is born with a serious birth defect or illness. In a healthy relationship, both partners work together to make the good times great and the bad times better.

What comes to your mind when you think of married life?

- Romantic dinners by candlelight
- Dancing until the wee small hours of the morning
- Walking hand-in-hand along lonely, moon-kissed beaches
- Taking trips together to exotic destinations

Hopefully, every marriage will include its share of such romantic moments. But these are not likely to be the day-to-day ingredients of any relationship, no matter how happy it is. Instead, marriage involves:

- Dealing with the daily routine of getting out of bed and going to work, doing the housework, fixing meals, etc., day after day after day
- Taking care of your spouse when he or she is sick
- Trying to stay on top of bills
- Devoting your weekend to working on household repairs when you'd rather be out doing something fun and exciting

And then, when children come along there's:

- Changing diapers
- Walking the floor with sick babies

- Cleaning up after sick babies
- Helping with homework
- Attending PTA meetings and back-to-school nights

In other words, a marriage is not likely to be one long party, and in a healthy relationship both partners understand and accept this. They know that for every hour spent walking along a moonlit beach together, there will probably be several hours of pushing a shopping cart down the aisle of a crowded supermarket, of rushing around in the morning to get ready for work, of cooking, cleaning, repairing, and doing all of the things that are a normal part of daily life. Marriage doesn't free you from any of these things, but it does give you a partner to help you shoulder the load, and if you work together in love the load will be lighter for both of you.

The healthy couple also has realistic expectations regarding the fact that there will be changes throughout the course of their relationship. They understand that there will periodically be the need to reexamine daily routines and renegotiate previous agreements and expectations.

For example, shortly before our daughter Darcie was born, Cindy approached me and requested that we make some changes with regard to the way we handled our laundry: Namely, she had been doing it all, and she wanted me to pitch in and help her with it. I readily agreed that hers was a reasonable request (no matter what *she* might tell you—especially the part about how it took me over a year and a half to incorporate her request into my daily routine).

A HEALTHY SEX LIFE

Sex isn't the be-all and end-all of marriage, but it's certainly important—for men *and women.*

A few years ago, advice columnist Ann Landers polled her readers regarding their feelings toward sex. She invited them to write and let her know whether or not sex was important to them. Well, she was flooded with letters from people—women, mostly—saying that sex wasn't important at all. By a large majority, these people said they would rather read, watch television, work in the garden, and a long list of other activities than make love.

I had two immediate responses to this. First, I realized that the responses she got are not necessarily representative of the way most people feel. After all, those who are angry and dissatisfied are much more likely to take the time to write a letter than are those who are happy and contented. For example, if you stay in a hotel and everything goes well, then you're not likely to write the manager to express your gratitude. But if the staff is rude, the air-conditioning doesn't work, the linens are soiled, and the mattress is lumpy—well then, you're probably going to write and tell the manager exactly how you feel. For that reason, I'm not sure the letters Ann Landers got are a true reflection of the feelings of the general public.

My second reaction is that the outpouring of negative feelings about sex represents a great tragedy, because it shows that there are many thousands of people who don't really understand sexual love. They see it as an act, as something mechanical, as a means of trying to find a little pleasure for oneself, but they don't see it as the natural physical expression of what has already happened in the hearts and souls of a man and a woman. That's what the sexual act is all about. It is a physical joining together of two people who have already been joined together emotionally and spiritually.

Our society uses sex in ways God never intended for it to be used.

For example, sex sells—everything from automobiles to beer and cigarettes. Go to your local newsstand and look at the covers of the magazines there. Many of them will be trying to outdo each other in terms of having the sexiest covers, and I'm not talking about magazines like *Playboy* and *Penthouse*.

Publishers of women's magazines, men's magazines, fitness magazines, travel magazines, adventure magazines, and news magazines all understand that sex sells, and all of them use it.

Go to any bookstore and you're sure to find several books telling you how to get the most from your sex life. Such books are full of suggestions on technique and positioning, but very few of them get down to the basic truth about sex, which is that it is one of life's greatest experiences when, and only when, it is shared with the one you truly love.

Many men and boys know that sex feels good, and so they lie and use women and girls to get what they want. They don't care how it is for the females they use, or how much they might be scarred physically or psychologically.

We have women and girls realizing that they can use sex to get what they want out of life. Some of them wind up openly selling their bodies on our city streets, while others use their sexuality to dig for gold in more "legal" ways. People use sex as a toy, as a diversion, as a means of getting what they want out of life, and that's wrong!

What I'm saying is that sex is one of God's greatest gifts to humankind, a wonderful expression of the love that one man and one woman feel for each other—a man and a woman who have pledged their lives to one another. Sadly, it is almost always true that Satan takes the utmost delight in sabotaging and twisting the greatest of God's gifts, and that is exactly what he has done with sex.

The healthy couple understands and appreciates sex for what it is—a loving physical expression of the love and closeness they feel for each other. For them, sex tends to be a happy expression of tenderness, affection, sexuality, passion, love, and playfulness. Each partner is involved in the act as a caring participant rather than as a passive receiver or an emotionally detached observer.

In these relationships, sex is not used as a weapon or a bribe. The wife doesn't deny her husband to get even with him for something he did that made her angry, nor does the husband tenderly make love to his wife because he is trying to get her to the point where she'll let him buy that new set of golf clubs he's had his eye on.

Optimally, sex always is an act of love and communication.

One other thing sex isn't, is a means for smoothing over other problems in a relationship. Some people seem to think that hopping into bed is the best way to overcome any marital difficulty and that's just not so. There are times when talking and working things out between you can be much more productive than making love. Certainly, engaging in the sex act can help you both forget your problems for a while, but it will not solve them and they will resurface sooner or later.

Oftentimes, premarital couples use sexual compatibility to reduce the anxieties raised due to conflict in other areas of their relationship. They seem to think, "We must be right for each other because we just had a great time in bed." But as I mentioned earlier, sex isn't the be-all and end-all of a romantic relationship, and there are other areas that are just as important, and perhaps even more important, than a healthy sex life.

Finally, in the area of sex, I have to say that healthy couples realize that their sexual relationship will evolve and change over time.

I knew of a young couple who put a quarter in a jar every time they made love. At the end of their first year of marriage they had enough money in that jar to pay for a weekend trip to an expensive resort. At the end of the second year, they had enough money for dinner at a fancy restaurant. At the end of the third year they were able to go out for burgers and fries at McDonald's.

I think they were exaggerating slightly, but I'm not sure.

The truth is that you cannot expect things to remain constant in the sexual arena. I'm not saying that sexual activity is necessarily going to diminish. It may actually increase. One partner's sexual appetite may increase while the other partner's appetite decreases. There will be other factors that will change a couple's sexual patterns—things like financial and job pressures, the introduction of children into the marriage, illness, etc. But here, as in every other area of a relationship, what is required is love, patience, understanding, and communication.

A SHARED SPIRITUAL COMMITMENT

More and more members of the mental health profession these days—Christians and non-Christians alike—

agree that the healthiest couples are those who share similar spiritual beliefs. I'm talking about spiritual beliefs that are relevant and practical to everyday life. In other words, beliefs that make a difference in the daily decisions these couples make, and in how they go about life on a regular basis—beliefs that help them discover who they are and that give meaning to their existence.

The healthiest couples believe that their existence matters and they have a deep and abiding sense of meaning and purpose in their lives.

Finally, their beliefs help reconcile them in a positive way to the passage of time and the inevitability of their own deaths.

So there we have some of the hallmarks of a healthy couple.

Coming up next, I'm going to discuss how people go about the process of choosing a life partner.

Don't go away.

Six

Choosing the Love of Your Life

Why do people get married?
You might be surprised.

There are many, many reasons, and very few of them have to do with "love" or "romance." In fact, the idea of marrying someone because you have fallen in love with him or her is rare—unheard of, even—in many parts of the world. Throughout Asia, for instance, many marriages are still arranged by the mothers and fathers of the prospective couple, and on some occasions, the bride has never even seen her husband before her wedding day.

And, even in what we might consider to be more "enlightened" parts of the world, the notion of marrying for love is a fairly recent one. I'm not saying that love is a modern invention. That would be preposterous, of course. The capacity to love another human being in a passionate, romantic way has always been part of human nature. That's the way God made us. I believe that one of the greatest love stories of all time can be found right there in Genesis, the first book of the Bible.

I'm talking about the marriage of Jacob and Rachel. If you're familiar with the story, you know that Jacob worked fourteen years to "earn" Rachel's hand in marriage. Fourteen years! The folks who run jewelry stores tell us that a diamond engagement ring ought to cost the prospective groom two months' salary, however much that is, and that sounds like a lot of money to most of us. (We should all be thankful they didn't say that the appropriate amount was two *years'* salary—which certainly would make millionaires out of most of those jewelers in no time at all.) But Jacob worked for Rachel for fourteen long years!

You don't work that long to get someone to marry you because you like the way she looks. After all, there's going to be a pretty big difference in the way someone looks after fourteen years anyway. No, it had to be love, and a pretty amazing kind of love at that.

And then, of course, we all know about the passionate (although fictional) love affair between Romeo and Juliet, and that was more than three hundred years ago.

So again, romantic love isn't anything new, but the idea that marriage exists primarily because of romantic love *is* new, relatively speaking.

But if you talk about love, the next thing you have to ask is, "What makes people fall in love?" And then, "How can I find the one who's out there waiting for me?"

Well . . . some people have the idea that God has designed this universe so that for every woman there is one special man, and for every man there is one special woman—a perfect match made in heaven. Do I believe that? I'm not sure. All I can say is that if it is true, there are an awful lot of people in this world who didn't look hard enough for their perfect mates. The divorce rate attests to that, as does the continuing high rate of spouse abuse.

On the other hand, there are many couples who seem to be "made for each other." It's always exciting to see two people come together who seem to mesh well in many ways. I certainly believe that marriage is an institution honored by God, but I also believe—even though some people may want to accuse me of heresy—that there are likely to be several wise and godly fits for you. There are those who would complement you beautifully, whose strengths and weaknesses would mesh very well with your own to make both of you much stronger as a couple than you could ever be as individuals.

If you're looking for a mate, I hope that what I'm saying doesn't distress you. I mean for it to be an encouragement. What I'm saying, after all, is that you don't have to scour the face of the earth looking for the one and only, "perfect" love of your life. Wherever you are, in a huge city or a tiny town, in a place where there are literally millions of potential mates to choose from, or in an area where eligible bachelors and bachelorettes are about as rare as pimples on Christie Brinkley's chin, someone right there could be just right for you. All you have to do is find that person (and eventually convince him or her that you are just right as well).

In this chapter I'm going to explain some of the relevant factors that affect and limit your options in the search for a spouse, and I'll take you through the process most people go through before they finally settle on one person with whom they want to spend the rest of their lives.

You know, it's really pretty startling when you think about it. There are billions of people on this planet, and your job is to pick one special person, out of all those billions of possibilities, to go through life with you. It would be terribly scary to think that out of all those millions of people there was only one correct choice. You'd have something like 1.5 billion chances of making a wrong decision, and only one chance of making the right one! That would mean that you'd have a better chance of winning the state lottery than of finding the "love of your life."

Don't despair, though, because before we've finished with this chapter, I'm going to give you some tools to help you make a wise decision in this all-important matter, and we'll discuss the factors that usually come into play in any search for a life partner.

Before we discuss those factors, a small word of encouragement. If you've been looking for Mr. or Miss Right for some time, and have come to feel that the odds of ever finding that perfect match are stacked against you . . . well, you're wrong. The odds aren't against you at all. It's just a matter of knowing how and where to look for him or her. And besides, even if those odds *were* stacked against you, you're pretty good when it comes to beating the odds anyway. After all, chances were about one in 30 trillion that you would ever be born.

Now, let's look at the factors that are involved in finding the Love of Your Life.

GEOGRAPHIC PROXIMITY

This makes sense.

You can't marry someone if you never have a chance to meet him or her. In other words, you won't find a young woman from Beverly Hills, California, marrying a Dinka tribesman from the interior of Kenya because they're just not likely to bump into each other at the corner grocery store, nor attend the same singles group at church.

Another way geography enters into the equation is that the population of your community determines whether you have many or few perspective partners. In other words, the single person who lives in New York or Chicago has a much greater "pool" from which to choose than does the single person who lives out in the middle of the desert—say, in Desert Center, California (population two hundred). Because people who live in more remote rural areas have fewer potential partners to choose from, some experts believe this helps to account for the fact that there are more early marriages and fewer divorces per capita in rural counties. For example, only 1.6 percent of women and 4.7 percent of men who live on farms have been divorced, as compared to many times that for the general population.

Another geographic factor that plays a role in the selection process is the ratio of men to women in a particular area. For example, an acquaintance just returned from a cruise to Alaska. While there, he met a woman from a tiny village in the northern part of the state, and he asked her how she liked living there.

"Are you kidding?" she asked, flashing a grin that revealed a mouth full of broken and crooked teeth. "I love it! Why, in Alaska there are a lot more men than women. Here, even *I* have a date *every* Saturday night."

Well, according to what I heard, the woman was certainly no dazzling beauty—not the kind of gal who was going to attract a man by her looks. But because of her geographic location, in a small Alaskan town where the men far outnumbered the women, she had a pretty fair chance of finding a date or, if she was interested, a husband. She has a large number of potential prospects to choose from. Who wouldn't tell her, "Go north, young woman"?

LEGAL AND MORAL CONSIDERATIONS

The second factor that enters into the search for a lifetime partner is whether or not the potential marriage would be legal and moral. I certainly don't want to belabor this point, because I feel confident that few people reading this book want to marry their aunt, uncle, cousin, grandmother or grandfather—but I've seen enough afternoon television to know that some pretty weird things happen on this planet of ours.

Not long ago I heard of a show wherein—let me see if I can get this straight—a young man had married his brother's wife's stepgrandmother, thereby making him his brother's stepgrandfather. I'm not really sure I got that right, but it was something like that, and I know that if you ever watch Donahue, Oprah, Geraldo, Montel, or any of the other folks who seem to rule over the airwaves from noon to five every day, you've got some pretty outrageous stories of your own to tell.

If you're an old-timer, you probably remember when rock 'n' roller Jerry Lee Lewis got in all sorts of hot water because he married his cousin. Not only was she his cousin, she was also thirteen years old!

Anyway, it may have been legal to marry a thirteen-year-old girl (who happened to be your cousin) in some part of the U.S. back then, but it isn't today. There are a number of laws that restrict who can marry whom . . . and I think that's enough to say about it.

PHYSICAL ATTRACTION

The third factor that enters into the search for a mate is whether or not there is a physical attraction. And that shouldn't be a surprise to anyone! This is the first of the factors that you can control. In other words, you probably can't do anything about geography—unless you're a single woman who can pack up and move to Alaska—and you can't do anything about the legal and moral factors related to marriage. But you *can* do something about picking someone you'd like to look at across the breakfast table for the rest of your life.

Whether it's right or wrong, wise or unwise, almost all single people go through what might be called a "visual elimination test" when they meet an unattached member of the opposite sex. If you like the way a person looks, you'll probably want to spend the time to get to know him better. If you don't like the way he looks, then you probably won't spend any time getting to know him. Of course, that's unfortunate, because how a person looks has nothing at all to do with who he is or what he's like. But still, physical attraction is important.

I remember an early episode of the old television show, *Cheers*, in which the well-educated and "enlightened" Diane Chambers wanted to prove to her friends that appearance wasn't important to her. And so, she began dating a man who was perfect for her in every way. He was bright, well-read, witty, caring, sensitive—all the things any

— 100 —

woman would want in a man. But he wasn't very good looking. In the end, and much to her own embarrassment, she had to admit that, yes, looks were important to her, and she broke off the relationship.

That's how it is in this physical-oriented world. Even those of us who realize that looks aren't everything still don't want to be married to someone we're just not attracted to.

Now it's true that beauty is pretty much in the eye of the beholder. Thankfully, we are not all attracted to the same type of person. The one you think of as beautiful or handsome, I might see as plain or homely. Physical beauty is a subjective thing, and that's why some tribesmen in Africa go to great length to stretch their necks, or to increase the size of their lips. Still, there are certain "attractive" characteristics that almost all of us look for in a mate, and one of those has to do with age. Most of us want to be married to someone who is fairly close to our own age.

Yes, I know that there are quite a few May-December marriages, and some of them have been successful, but it's not easy to make that type of marriage work.

SOCIOECONOMIC CLASS

Social class is the single most powerful social variable determining the choice of a mate. People will tend to marry outside their race, religion, age or ethnic group before they will go outside of their socioeconomic status boundaries.

Real life doesn't have very many stories of poverty-stricken Cinderellas winding up married to Prince Charmings, and despite what Billy Joel sang a few years ago, most uptown girls are not going to wind up married to down-town guys.

People tend to stay within their social class because background has a whole lot to do with who you are as a person. It has to do with education, occupation, values, tastes, attitudes, and so on. People of the same class will be much more likely to "speak the same language" and relate on the same level.

For example, some people would feel out of place in an elegant restaurant with linen tablecloths, candles on the tables, and food with fancy names that require a complete knowledge of all Romance languages. They wouldn't know which fork or which dish to use first. They're "steak and potatoes" kind of people who feel more at home in a diner, a cafeteria, or a place where they use the proverbial phrase, "Would you like an order of fries with that?"

At the same time, there are those who feel completely at ease in the most elegant surroundings. Their manners are impeccable and they have every one of the social graces. They are never guilty of committing a single faux pas. And yet, take those same people to Burger King and they might feel completely at a loss. They don't want to be snobs, you understand. They just don't know how to behave in a relaxed, informal atmosphere.

All of this has to do with socioeconomic class. And so, although it might sound "snooty" to say that social class matters, the fact is that it *does* matter very much. People rarely marry outside of their social class because it is just not likely to be a comfortable fit. A marriage of this kind— say, between a banker's daughter who's graduated from Sarah Lawrence, and the uneducated son of a factory worker—will have to overcome some serious challenges if it's going to work.

PERSONAL VALUES

Now we get to the more serious matters.

Once a person has passed through the more superficial filters of attractiveness and social class, deeper evaluations begin to take place. These evaluations are meant to determine how another person's self, status, beliefs, and values match up with your own. The major values relevant to this evaluation process are listed below.

Religion

As recently as twenty-five years ago, interfaith marriages were fairly rare. However, in the late 1960s, social taboos against such marriages began to weaken, and today, fully one-third of all American marriages cut across religious lines (i.e., Catholic-Protestant, Christian-Jewish, etc.).

Still, for many people, and especially those who are serious about their faith, it is vitally important to find a partner who believes the same things they believe.

Even in relationships where both partners are from the same religion, or even the same denomination, there can be considerable room for individual differences in terms of an understanding of God, how one views the Bible, and an involvement in formal religious activities. But a marriage between a born-again Christian and someone who doesn't even believe in Christ is likely to be stressful and difficult right from the start.

If you are a Christian who is considering marriage, or even a serious relationship, with a non-Christian, please think again about the Bible's warning not to be unequally yoked with an unbeliever. The person who thinks, "I'll go ahead and marry him now, and then I can always lead him to Christ later on," is not being realistic. There's no guarantee that it will ever happen. And I've seen too many instances where it *didn't* happen.

Although the specific divorce rates vary depending upon the particular religions involved, overall, interfaith marriages have been shown to have significantly higher divorce rates than same-faith unions. In his book, *The Psychology of Religion: An Empirical Approach* (New York: Prentice Hall, 1985), Bernard Spilka says that a series of studies on Catholic-Protestant marriages found divorce rates that were two to five times greater than were true of marriages within those separate faiths. The highest divorce rate of all was found among Catholics who had married those who had no religious affiliation. A study of Jewish-Christian mixed marriages found a divorce rate nearly six times higher than when both partners are Jewish. Apparently, it's not easy to make a go of it in a marriage that involves mixing religions.

Life Goals

Do you know what you want out of life? What your goals are? Where you're headed?

It's important to know these things, and it's also important to know your potential partner's goals as well, so you can make certain that what you want and what your partner wants are compatible. I'm sure that seems obvious enough. If your goal is to buy some land out in the country and raise cattle, but the love of your life wants to buy a condo right in the heart of the city—then you might have a tad of trouble getting those goals to mesh.

Now when you're in the state of being dazzled by the light of romance, that might not seem like such a big deal. "Well, maybe I'll just keep a few cows on the roof." But as time goes by, such a situation is likely to lead to terrible resentment, as in, "I gave up my dream for you, and what did it get me?"

It's unfortunate that many prospective couples, perhaps even most of them, never talk about their long-range goals and plans. They just naturally assume that because they love each other, everything will fit together and work out. But it's a mistake to think that your partner is just naturally going to come into line with your plans, or you with his or hers.

It's not so important that your goals be identical, but things go much smoother the more similar they are. If they are mutually exclusive, you are heading for big-time problems.

Some of the areas where you need to make sure that you and your partner's goals line up are:

- Will you be career- or family-oriented?
- Do you want to live in the quietness of the countryside or in the noise and excitement of the city?
- Do you hope to have children, and if so, how many?
- What sort of lifestyle do you want? In other words, do you expect to live in a nice house and drive a fancy car? How much do you need in order to be satisfied?
- What are your goals with regard to your church and community? Do you aspire to positions of leadership? Are you a "joiner" or a "non-joiner?"

It may be possible that you've never given a great deal of thought to your long-range goals. If you haven't, it's never too late—or too early—to start. Take a few hours or a day to think about where you want your life to go. Get out a piece of paper and write down your long-term and short-term goals. Such an exercise will help you see the "big picture" of your life, and can help you devise a plan to get you where you want to go. In other words, until you know the destination you want, there's no way to draw up a road map to get you there.

Politics

Politics is the third area where alignment of personal values is important to a marriage.

A little while ago we talked about a couple who has managed to build a lasting marriage even though their politics are diametrically opposed. That's rare. Most of the time people feel as passionate about their politics as they do about their religion, and mixing political views can be as explosive as combining the letters T-N-T.

Some combinations which aren't likely to work very well include liberal–conservative, activist–apathetic, and Democrat–Republican. Again, I'm not saying that a marriage featuring mixed politics won't work and work well. I am saying that these are some areas that ought to be considered before your organist plays the first few notes of "The Wedding March." And, of course, the stronger your political feelings are, the more important it is for you to find a partner who feels the same way.

Sex

Do you and your partner share the same views about sex? This is important, not only in a marriage, but also in the period leading up to the marriage. An engaged couple constantly faces questions about their own sexual relationship. The main question is, "How far should we go?" "Is it okay to engage in sexual intercourse now that we're engaged to each other?" In the stereotypical situation, the man is pushing the woman to "give in" to him, and she's trying hard to "hold out."

There was a time when the stereotype had a lot of validity, and in some instances it still does. But society's attitudes toward sex have changed. Women are more aggressive when it comes to sex. They know what they want and they expect satisfaction.

There was a time when every young girl wanted to be thought of as a virgin, even if she wasn't. It was important for her to keep a good reputation. Unfortunately, in today's society, most girls of high school and college age *don't* want to be thought of as virgins, even if they are, because it's bad form to be pure. How unfortunate that our world has turned in that direction.

But really, purity, celibacy, and "saving yourself" for marriage will always be the wisest choice, even if such decisions are considered out of style. That's the best view to have, even now. Engaging in sex prior to marriage can cause all sorts of problems, especially for Christians, and in my office I'm sure that I've seen just about all of them.

One of those problems stems from the fact that an engagement is just that, an engagement, and not a marriage. Engagements can be and often are broken. When that happens, the young man and woman who were engaging in sexual intercourse because "We're just as good as married," may suddenly find themselves with a couple of tons of guilt to carry around every day. They may feel used, or "ruined," and be filled with regret.

Having the same values and understanding with regard to sex is very important to the over-all success of a marriage. It's not always easy to talk about sex. It can be embarrassing. But it must be done, because sex is so important, and always will be.

Spouses or POSSLQs?

Since American society has become more liberal over the past twenty-five years or so, one of the dilemmas involving values that any serious couple must face is whether or not they really want to be married to each other. In our society, thousands of men and women are deciding that they would rather live together without benefit of marriage. Because these couples cannot formally be categorized as spouses by the United States Census Bureau, they have in the past been classified as "POSSLQs" pronounced "possel-cues," which stands for "Persons of Opposite Sex Sharing Living Quarters." Some people would never consider marriage without first giving it a "trial run." Unfortunately, for those choosing to undertake such a trial, this arrangement may be ruining their chances for marital happiness. Studies have shown that marriages which eventually grow out of a "POSSLQ" arrangement have a significantly higher divorce rate than marriages that are *not* preceded by a period of nonmarried cohabitation.

It really isn't a very good idea. It doesn't work all that well. And it seems to me to be contrary to God's perfect will for His people.

So there you have five of the most important personal values that go into the building of a successful marriage.

Now let's take a look at the next "filter" that a relationship must pass through on its way to becoming a marriage.

ROLE COMPATIBILITY

At a fairly early stage in their relationship, a dating couple usually reaches the point where both partners are thinking, "Okay, I know a lot about you and so far I haven't seen anything that would rule you out as a potential mate. But what I still don't know is how well we fit together as a couple."

You see, some people are so much alike that they are not a good fit. They have the same strengths and the same weaknesses, and even many of the same abilities and talents. The result is that their life together is likely to resemble a competition more than a partnership. Because they are both strong in the same areas, they may wind up trying to outdo each other, and because they are both weak in the same areas they will not be able to help lift each other up during times of stress or trouble that come their way.

On the other hand, some people are so different that there is no way for them to be a comfortable fit. They have very little in common, and their personalities are at the opposite ends of the spectrum. The result is that as soon as the glow of new love begins to fade, they start driving each other absolutely crazy. They quickly get to the point where the very sound of the other's voice has all the charm and attraction of a set of fingernails being scraped across a chalkboard.

But then there are those couples who just seem to fit together perfectly. Not too much alike. Not too different. When he's weak, she helps him to be strong, and vice versa.

When she sees the bad side of something and gets depressed about it, he's able to see the possible positive outcome and cheer her up. They just fit together like the pieces of a jigsaw puzzle.

What makes the "perfect" couple? One of the most important things is an understanding of the roles each person will have in the relationship. The main issues to be considered in this area are: Are we equals in this relationship? Do we really have the same rights and privileges or does one party tend to dominate? Does one party tend to submit to the other in a "whipped-puppy" type of way?

Let's look at some of the areas where role compatibility is important.

Decision making and problem solving. How are you going to make the major decisions that will confront you as a couple? Will you talk directly and honestly to each other, respecting each other's feelings and thoughts—always being willing to compromise for the sake of a healthy relationship? Or will everything be done through power plays, manipulation, or other less direct and less healthy methods? In some marriages, one of the partners "allows" the other to make all the small decisions, while reserving the right to make all of the "big ones" for himself. But a marriage simply will not work if one of the spouses makes all of those big decisions such as where the family will go for vacation this year, what kind of a car they will drive, which neighborhood they will live in, etc.

"Now, let's see, you decided on which movie we went to on Saturday night, so I get to choose where we'll go for our two-week vacation this year. And you decided which kind of cereal to buy at the grocery store, so I get to decide what kind of a car we're going to drive!"

No . . . "shared" decision making like that just isn't going to cut it.

Now it could be that you're saying, "I really don't know whether my intended will try to make all of the decisions for me. How can I tell?" Well, when you're dining out together, does he (or she) tend to suggest, very strongly, what you should order? I'm not talking about giving advice in regard to your questions, but about taking over and telling you what to do. When the waiter comes to your table and asks you if everything is all right, does your partner quickly say, "Oh, yes, everything is great," without giving you a chance to react? Is your opinion ever considered? When you're going out on a date, do you decide where to go, or does your partner *always* make the decision?

If your partner is making all of the decisions for you now—even if those decisions are in relatively small, insignificant areas of life—you can bet that he'll want to keep making up your mind for you after you're married. Is that what you want? I sure hope it's not.

Leisure and recreation. Do you like to do the same things for rest and relaxation? Really? Many a young woman has tried to convince herself that she likes to do the things her boyfriend likes to do, when she'd really much rather do just about anything else. I've talked to women who have put worms on fishhooks, cleaned fish, gone camping, devoted themselves to football, and taken on a number of other "manly" pursuits in the name of love. For the sake of fairness, I have to say that I've also met some men who have developed a sudden interest in art museums, romantic movies and so on, because they were trying to capture a lady's attention.

But ask yourself if you are going to be happy baiting hooks, cleaning fish, and attending football games for the rest of your life. Are you going to continue to be delighted with art shows and romantic films?

And there are other things to think about. What hobbies do you have, and how important are they to you? Are you a "party" person, or would you rather stay at home and watch TV? Are you athletically inclined, or someone who has no interest at all in sports?

One premarital couple I was counseling was having a particularly difficult time because the man was very much into outdoor activities like rock climbing and backpacking, while the woman was much more sedate and enjoyed such activities as working on crafts, ceramics, quilting, and the like.

If you are not compatible in these important areas of life, then you can be sure that your relationship is going to take compromise and hard work.

Husband and wife roles. Compatibility is important in your understanding of husband and wife roles. There are far fewer predetermined "husband and wife" roles now than ever before. It used to be unheard of, for example, for a man to stay home and run the house while his wife went to work and earned the living. That's still rare today, but it is considered an acceptable alternative instead of deviant behavior. In many other areas of life today, people are free to be who they are rather than being limited to narrow, specific roles because of their gender. And this is good.

But there is a downside to this freedom as well, and that is that there is often a confusion about who will assume which duties within the marriage. Twenty-five or thirty years ago, the roles of husband and wife were fairly clearly defined. Each knew what was expected of them, and each knew what they expected of the other.

Today's couple is faced with many questions regarding who will handle which responsibility. For example:

- Who will be the main provider?
- Will one be the primary caretaker of the children?
- Which partner will take on the traditional "male" tasks of household maintenance, car upkeep, yard work, and so on?
- Which partner will take on the traditional female role of housekeeper, cook, nurturer, etc.?

It is important to have a clear understanding in all of these areas.

The next area of role compatibility doesn't have much to do with your relationship with each other. It has to do with, dare I say it, in-laws. Believe me when I tell you that a great many marriages have been destroyed by meddling in-laws, or, just as often, by husbands or wives who were antagonistic toward their spouse's family. (Contrary to what you might hear, it's not always the mother-in-law's fault.)

It's not easy to develop a good relationship with your in-laws, and that's precisely why there are so many good one-liners related to them—and mothers-in-law specifically. For example, Jill Bauer, in *From "I Do" to "I'll Sue,"* notes this one from Sholem Aleichem: "The luckiest man was Adam—he had no mother-in-law. " And Bauer records this negative sentiment from Sir Geoffrey Wrangham, a justice and specialist in divorce cases for the British High

Court during the 1960s: "Distrust all mothers-in-law. They are completely unscrupulous in what they say in court. The wife's mother is always more prejudiced against the husband than even the most ill-treated wife. If I had my way, I am afraid I would abolish all mothers-in-law entirely" (New York: Plume-Meridian, 1993).

PSYCHOLOGICAL AND INTRAPSYCHIC FACTORS

We've taken a look at quite a few of the steps involved in the selection of a lifetime partner (or perhaps, more accurately, we've looked at a number of ways in which prospective partners can be eliminated from consideration). We've talked about the filters of proximity, legal restrictions, personal attraction, socioeconomic class, life values, and role compatibility. Once a person has met most or all of your standards in these areas, the next thing to consider is their internal psychological makeup, and, specifically, how well the attributes and needs of their psyche match up with your own intrapsychic strength and needs.

I realize that some of this may sound like psychobabble. But bear with me, because it's important, and in the next few pages I'm going to explain why.

Complementarity

I want to consider an important and age-old question: Is it really true that opposites attract, or is it the other way around? Are people attracted to each other, instead, because they are so much alike?

It does seem to be true that people are often attracted to others whose personalities are different from, but complementary to, their own. Although there is not a great deal of research to support this contention, it also seems that such "complementary" couples are often able to build successful, lasting relationships.

Harville Hendrix, author of *Getting the Love You Want* (New York: Harper Collins, 1990) and *Keeping the Love You Find* (New York: Pocket Books, 1992), believes that one of the reasons we are attracted to certain people is because they make up for or complete our personalities in the traits that we were taught to repress as children. I think that's probably true. I also believe that our partner's strengths may complete us in the areas we simply never developed, for whatever reason. For example, if I am totally disorganized, one of those people who spend at least an hour every day looking for something I've misplaced— then I may be seriously attracted to someone who lives life by the axiom "a place for everything and everything in its place."

Let's take a look at a few of the complementary "opposites" that might go together.

The introvert and the extrovert. I'm sure you've seen this "odd couple." One of them is the life of the party, telling jokes and carrying on, perhaps getting out the old guitar and belting out a few choruses from Saturday Night Fever or some such classic. Meanwhile, the other one is content to sit in the shadows, far away from the spotlight, quietly sipping a drink and hoping that the party will soon be over.

Actually, this combination can work well, as long as the introverted partner isn't inwardly jealous of the ease with which his partner commands center stage. If the introvert is content to let his partner "shine," and if the extrovert doesn't feel compelled to try to drag his partner into the spotlight with him, then the two of them will do just fine, thank you.

It is also true that each of these people can directly benefit and grow from the other's natural tendencies. The extrovert can model for his partner that it is not so hard to reach out of yourself and interact more freely with all kinds of people. The more inwardly-oriented partner can help the extrovert expand his self-understanding and teach him the value of introspection. The quiet partner often gets vicarious pleasure watching his more expressive mate interact with people so easily. The louder partner may enjoy the benefit of the calming influence his beloved can have on him. (And he may also enjoy having someone around who always seems willing to sit back and enjoy his "performance.")

The realist and the dreamer. Put two dreamers together and they're likely to dream their way right into the poorhouse. Put two "realists" together, and life may become a worrisome drudgery. You've got to be free to dream, but you've also got to keep at least one foot on the solid ground of reality.

The realist is someone who is good with facts and details, someone who's not afraid to face up to difficulties and develop real solutions. The realist is someone who looks down the road to see what's coming, and then gets prepared for its arrival. These are the strengths the dreamer needs. He needs someone to help him deal with the realities of the here and now, to read the fine print on the contract, and to focus on what joys can be derived from this present moment.

On the other side of the coin, the dreamer tends to have an enthusiasm and creativity that may be lacking in the life of the realist. He can help his partner get excited about the possibilities of life.

As an example of how the dreamer and the realist might work together, it would be the dreamer who would come up with some great idea, but the realist would be the one who would do what was necessary to turn that idea into a reality. In other words, the dreamer is the one who sees the big picture, while the realist is the one who deals with all the smaller details.

Again, this isn't a bad combination, so long as the two partners do not attempt to remake each other into their own images.

The thinker and the feeler. This can be another good combination if both partners are willing to learn from each other.

Feelers are generally guided by emotion, and are especially known for basing all of their decisions on how those decisions might affect other people. Sometimes, in fact, we can become so concerned about how our decisions will affect other people that it's hard for us to make any decisions at all. After all, it is a very rare decision that pleases everyone, that doesn't hurt someone in one way or another. Now, notice that I'm saying "we" about feelers, and that's on purpose because, yes, I *am* a feeler, and, what's more, a feeler who happens to be married to a woman who is very much a thinker.

What are "thinkers" like? In the extreme, this individual is guided by logic and "the bottom line." The world's foremost thinker, in fact, is undoubtedly Mr. Spock, the Vulcan of *Star Trek* fame. If you know anything about *Star Trek*, (and who in twentieth-century America doesn't?) you know that Mr. Spock is guided solely by what is "logical."

If something doesn't make sense, it just doesn't compute in Spock's brain, and he is continually perplexed by the fact that we earthlings base so many of our decisions on nothing more than emotion.

It's pretty easy to see, then, why the thinker needs the perspective the feeler can bring, and vice versa.

The feeler needs to see that there are other important things to consider besides feelings and emotions. He needs to see, in fact, that those who base all of their decisions on their feelings are often easy prey for those who want to take advantage of them.

The thinker, meanwhile, needs to see that the "human factor" is important, and that there are times when other considerations must take precedence over the bottom line on the ledger sheet.

Because we feelers are person-centered in our concerns and generally are fairly warm and sensitive, we're usually pretty good at teaching, selling, counseling, and cheerleading (such as conducting "positive thinking" seminars). But we often need others to help us organize, analyze, and weigh the evidence needed to make a proper decision. Because of our sensitive natures, if one of us is called upon to fire someone, we will worry and brood about it for days or weeks both before and after the incident, even if we know deep down inside that the person who was fired clearly deserved to be discharged.

Thinkers, on the other hand, usually excel in business, science, research, accounting, etc.

If you are interested in further research into personality types, I suggest you look into taking the Myers-Briggs Type Indicator. When my wife Cindy and I recently took this test we found that we are fairly extreme opposites. No wonder

we have so many interesting conversa
house!

If you'd like to do some additional reading on
subject of addressing and resolving temperament differences, I recommend Bill and Lynne Hybel's excellent book,
Fit to Be Tied (Grand Rapids: Zondervan, 1991), especially
the ninth chapter. Another excellent book is *Please Understand Me*, by Marilyn Bates and David Keirsey (Del Mar,
CA: Prometheus, 1984).

Homogeneity

Opposites do sometimes attract. But another psychological factor enters into our choice of a mate: *homogeneity.*

Statistics seem to suggest that this is important. They
show that your marriage will have a greater chance of
succeeding if you and your spouse are similar in specific
ways, including socioeconomic background, race, religion,
values, leisure interests, and the ways in which you view
the roles of male/female within a relationship and/or a
marriage.

Now, let me introduce you to yet another theory. It is
called "the equity/exchange theory," and what these fancy-
sounding words mean is that you will probably not feel
totally comfortable with your partner unless you have
obtained a fairly equal exchange with your beloved in most
of these areas.

In other words, you will just naturally feel more at ease
with a partner who is similar to you in level of attractiveness,
social status, educational background, and so on. If my
spouse were much "better" than me in some of these
areas—for instance, if she had a graduate degree while I had
dropped out of high school—I would probably feel bad

about the match, and believe that I wasn't contributing my fair share to the situation. And, if things were reversed and I had a far superior education, I might tend to look down on her and become condescending and patronizing. I might resent her for lagging so far behind me. I wouldn't do it on purpose, of course, but chances are good that a resentful, bitter attitude toward my partner would develop over time.

It's also true that we're usually most comfortable with someone whose general emotional and mental health is comparable to our own. (Remember that the next time you're tempted to wonder how your love interest could act so weird sometimes!)

Some of the areas where we want to be like our partner include:

Self-esteem. If you like yourself, and feel good about yourself, you're likely to be happier and get along with people better—including your partner. The weaker and more insecure you are, the more you're likely to mistrust people, to think the worst of them, and to isolate yourself from them. Two insecure people living under the same roof will have more difficulty getting along because they will each be more easily threatened, distort reality more frequently, and be less likely to communicate in healthy ways.

Unresolved emotional pain and trauma. It's also important to ask whether you or your potential partner has suffered from physical, verbal, emotional, and/or sexual abuse as a child, and if so, how far you have come along the road to recovery. Now it could be that we're not talking about anything that would qualify as "abuse," but about something as simple as growing up in a home where your parents had no idea how to express their love—for you, or for each other. That is the kind of thing that can cause continuing emotional pain. Often, you will find two "hurting" people getting together in a relationship based on their mutual neediness. Sadly, it's difficult to build a lasting relationship upon pain and need.

Identity formation. A person's overall level of psychological well-being, his ability to "function" in life, is strongly influenced by whether or not he has developed a mature adult identity. A person with such an identity is capable of conducting his own affairs. He can take care of his needs in terms of finances, living arrangements, finding friends, and so on. Essentially, the person who has developed a proper, mature identity doesn't need his parents, or anybody else, in order to function effectively. That doesn't mean he won't feel lonely or stressed-out at times. But for the most part, this person enjoys life and is a productive member of society.

The person who has not developed a mature identity may see himself as little more than an extension of his parents. He's never been able to cut those apron strings, and is dependent on his parents for his beliefs, values, and convictions. In other words, he's never come to see himself as an independent person who is capable of thinking and acting for himself. He can carry this sort of behavior into a romantic relationship in either of two ways, both of which can be destructive. First, he can continue to be emotionally dependent upon his mother and father instead of focusing his energies on building a new, strong relationship with his romantic partner. Second, he can transfer his feelings of dependency from his parents to his partner, thereby becoming a dependent, clinging, and, eventually, suffocating partner.

A WORD OF WARNING

So far we've been talking about personality differences and similarities that mesh together in a mutually beneficial way. But in order for any meshing to take place, both partners have to be willing to listen to and learn from each other. And both partners have to realize that there are strengths and weaknesses in every personality characteristic. If you think that your personality is the "correct" one and your partner's is "wrong," then you won't have much of a chance of building an effective partnership.

For example, there are strengths that come from being a dreamer, but there are also drawbacks. There are strengths associated with being a realist, but there are also negative aspects of that personality type. The idea here is for your love and respect for each other to keep you more in the center of things, balancing each other and keeping each other from getting too far out in any direction. In order for this to happen, you have to respect each other's views about life. If both of you are extreme in your views— for example, if you're a feeler who sees thinkers as being coldhearted and uncaring—then it's certainly not going to be a day at the beach if you should wind up married to one.

Another thing you probably ought to think about is that a personality characteristic that may appeal to you in small quantities may take on all the appeal of the black death when taken in larger doses. Suppose, for example, that you are rather disorganized, maybe even sloppy. You're lucky if you're able to balance your checkbook one month out of every year. If so, you may appreciate your partner's advice that helps you get your finances in order and enables you to balance your checkbook on a regular basis. But chances are that you're not going to appreciate it so much when your organized partner starts turning his or her attention to other areas of your life—such as how to arrange the items in your filing cabinet, how to keep your sock drawer organized, how to keep the items on your desk arranged, and so on. The person you once considered to be neat and organized may now be seen as a control freak and a royal pain the neck.

So what am I saying? Simply that you should be aware of the paradox. Some of the traits that you find so appealing and attractive right now may drive you up the wall later on!

You should also be aware of the fact that some people are attracted to each other because they complement each other in unhealthy ways. One example of this would be the person who is emotionally dependent, who has the need to be taken care of, and who might become involved with a hyper-responsible "rescuer" who needs to be needed. The extreme form of negative complementarity would be where one person has the need to dominate and hurt others and another person has the need to be dominated and hurt. Have you ever wondered why so many sweet, sensitive women seem to be attracted to men who are self-centered bullies? Often it is because these women think so poorly of themselves that they feel a "need" to suffer.

For example, I remember a beautiful young woman named Mary. She was bright, intelligent, witty, and had a smile so bright she could have stepped out of a toothpaste ad. But according to her boyfriend, Mary was just about worthless. He didn't know why he put up with her, and often told her so. She couldn't seem to do anything to please him, and there wasn't much about her that appealed to him. He told her that he only stayed with her because he felt sorry for her, and because nobody else would have her anyway.

It was only years later that Mary would admit to me that there was a part of her that enjoyed being abused by this jerk of a boyfriend. She thought she deserved to be treated that way, and in some way she felt that she was paying for her shortcomings.

When I delved into Mary's past, I discovered that she had been raised by a mother who could have given lessons in how not to raise a child. On occasion she had been physically violent. She frequently had been verbally violent. She had been a very negative woman who could never find it within herself to say anything like, "You did a good job," or "I'm proud of you," or "I love you." She had unwittingly taught Mary that she was virtually worthless as a human being, and so in her dating relationships Mary consistently sought out men who verified her own low opinion of herself. Whenever she dated a man who treated her well, as if she were a lady, she was uncomfortable, and found a reason to stop the relationship before it ever got started.

Fortunately, when Mary began to understand where her negative self-image came from she was able to to leave her boyfriend and conscientiously work to avoid entangling herself in unhealthy and abusive relationships. It wasn't all that easy for her to overcome her low self-esteem, but she agreed that she would always demand to be treated with respect, even on those days when she may have felt as if she didn't really deserve it. As she constantly struggled against her feelings of self-doubt and insecurity, Mary eventually came to see herself as someone worthy of love and respect, and she is no longer involved in an abusive relationship.

WHY YOU WANT TO MARRY YOUR MOM OR DAD—OR BOTH

Talking about Mary leads me to one of the most important psychological reasons for choosing a life-partner, which is: People very often choose someone who reminds them of one of their parents. (And not necessarily the opposite-sex parent.)

This is rarely done on purpose, and despite the lyrics of the old song, "I want a girl just like the girl who married dear old Dad," most people would cringe if you suggested to them that they had fallen in love with someone who reminded them of their mother or father. They'd cringe and shake their heads and say that it couldn't be true, even when it is true.

I believe this situation has little if anything to do with old Oedipus. It's not that you have some secret wish to marry your mother or father. It's just that, for various reasons, we tend to choose as our partners those who are an awful lot like our parents. For example, if Dad is an alcoholic, chances are very good that his little girl will grow up to marry an alcoholic. If Mom is a domineering, critical woman, then her son is likely to wind up with a domineering and critical wife.

I'm not suggesting that marrying someone who is like

your mother or father is always a negative thing. If your mom is a living saint, then you could do worse than marrying a girl who is just like her. Ditto if dear old Dad makes all those wise sitcom fathers look like so many flakes and loonies. But remember that it's important to take a look at your relationship with your parents, as well as your boyfriend's or girlfriend's relationship with his or her parents, before you go shopping for that wedding cake.

While it isn't immediately clear how a child's relationship with his parents in his formative years may eventually impact his choice of a spouse, more and more experts are coming to see that it does. One of the first to suggest that this is so was none other than Sigmund Freud.

Now if you were paying attention, you heard me say that it wasn't necessarily the characteristics of the opposite-sex parent that people look for in a partner. And you might ask, "You mean a woman might want to marry someone who reminds her of her mother—or a man someone who reminds him of his father?" That's right.

For example, in his book, *Beneath Mate Selection and Marriage: The Unconscious Motives in Human Pairing*, David Klimek argues that most people choose a spouse who reminds them either of their mother or father, and that this choice is based on a rather complicated interaction between the personality styles of the child and the parents, and upon which parent the child most closely identified with during his formative years (New York: VanNostrand Reinhold Company, 1979). Others believe that we simply tend to look for a mate who has the personality characteristics of the parent with whom we had the most conflict as a child, and with whom we have the most unresolved emotional baggage.

Some of the most recent thinking on this issue comes from Harville Hendrix, the author of *Getting the Love You Want* and *Keeping the Love You Find*. Hendrix's theories have been validated by the fact that he's been on *Oprah* five times. (If anyone's been on *Oprah* more than three times you just *gotta* believe him!) Hendrix believes that most people are attracted to someone who exhibits the main characteristics of *both* parents. He has come up with a word, *IMAGO*, which he says is an unconscious image of the opposite sex that we have been forming since birth. He states that it is a composite picture of the positive and negative personality traits of our primary caretakers. When the time comes for us to begin looking for a life-partner, we continue to look until we find someone who closely matches this *IMAGO*.

Although there are plenty of theories floating around as to why we tend to link up with people who remind us of our parents, all of these theories have two points in common. First, they agree that people who do this tend to choose someone who reminds them of significant emotional experiences that took place in their families during their growing-up years. And, second, most of these theories also maintain that the traits to which we are most strongly attracted tend to be the negative ones.

This is a huge point. In fact, if you've got a felt-tip marker handy, you might want to get it out and underline that last paragraph right now.

Think about it. What this means is that the average person may choose to commit his life to someone who embodies the primary negative characteristics of both of his or her parents.

Are you thinking that this doesn't makes sense?

No, it doesn't, at least not on the surface. But even though we humans like to believe that we are rational and thinking creatures, when you get down beneath the surface a little way you soon discover that many of the things we do are not based on logic or rational thinking at all.

But still, why would anyone want to fall in love with someone who had the worst characteristics of both of his parents?

I believe there are three reasons for this—one neutral, one positive, and one negative.

First, the neutral reason: A person may be drawn to recreate the negative tone of his childhood simply because this is what he is accustomed to and comfortable with. As in Mary's case, she is so used to being treated badly that it actually feels awkward and uncomfortable when someone treats her nicely.

Second, the positive reason: Which is that a person may be trying to make right in the present what was so wrong in the past. For example, by gaining the love and acceptance of a cold and distant love interest, I may be subconsciously trying to undo or make right the rejection and lack of acceptance I felt from my parents. This is positive because it is part of my striving for wholeness, health, and restitution. I may not be going about it the right way, but I am still striving to make my life better by righting old wrongs.

Third, the negative reason: Some people try to recapture the past because at some deep level they simply believe that they don't deserve any better. They have bought into the terrible lies that physical, sexual, and/or emotional abuse and neglect make children believe, namely, "I'm worthless. I'm nothing. All I'm good for is to meet someone else's perverted emotional or sexual needs." Since this person believes he deserves to be treated badly, he will subconsciously choose relationships with people who will treat him accordingly. What's more, if people don't treat him badly of their own accord, he may try to provoke their ill treatment. For example, the sharp-tongued, sarcastic wife who provokes her husband until he slaps or punches her may be subconsciously trying to get that reaction from him. She would probably deny it if you asked her, but if you looked beneath the surface that might very well be what you'd find.

Now, there is some good news here, and that is that the healthier and happier your childhood was, the less negative material you will have to draw upon when you are looking for a life partner. But still, even in the happiest childhood there are some negatives, and those negatives will exert the strongest pull on you as you look for the one with whom you want to spend the rest of your life.

So there you have some of the many reasons why people choose their partners. I know it's complicated. And I certainly don't expect you to get out a checklist and flip through it the first time you're out on a date with someone. At the same time, though, it is a very good idea to be aware of some of these subconscious factors that enter into the selection of a mate—and especially the negative ones so you may avoid them.

Coming up next, we'll talk about what it takes to become . . . well . . . intimate.

Seven

True Intimacy: It Don't Come Easy

Do you remember that great scene from the movie *Fiddler on the Roof*?

Tevye is feeling a little downhearted, and he wants to know if his wife loves him. He doesn't hint around about it, the way some of us would. He just asks her flat out, "Do you love me?"

And how does she answer?

"For thirty years I've ironed your shirts . . ."

"Do you love me?" he persists.

"For thirty years I've cleaned your house . . ."

"Do you love me?"

"For thirty years I've ironed your shirts, cleaned your

house, and cooked your meals . . . and you want to know if I love you?"

"Do you love me?"

Finally, the woman tells him what he wants to hear.

"Yes . . . I love you."

See, at first, she thinks that listing all of the things she does for him is enough. She tries to hide behind a "laundry list" of loving actions. But that won't do it. He wants to hear her express her love for him, and he won't be satisfied until she does.

What he wants, you see, is true intimacy. He needs her to break down the walls she's built around herself and open her heart to him.

It's sad but true that real intimacy is hard to come by. It's human nature to want to hold a little bit back, to think, "I don't want to reveal myself totally to you because that makes me vulnerable."

I have counseled couples who have lived in the same house for years, going to bed together every night, getting up together every morning, and yet who have never achieved true intimacy. Or . . . if they had it once upon a time, they've lost it.

So sad! Because it's so important to the health of any love relationship.

What does it mean to be "intimate" with someone? For the answer, let's turn to our old friend Webster who says that it means essential, belonging to, or characterizing one's deepest nature (Springfield, MA: Merriam Webster, 1988).

As you can see from this definition, intimacy is not something that comes easy, or overnight. It takes work, it takes perseverance, it takes patience, and it takes love to build a truly intimate relationship with another person.

Sadly, some people go through their entire lives without ever knowing what it means to have an intimate relationship. Some people cannot be intimate because they can't let another get that close to them. Others can't be intimate because they aren't capable of caring for another person in that way—or at least, won't let themselves care that much. This is largely the result of fear, fear that if I let you get too close to me, or if I get too close to you, I might wind up getting hurt.

This is generally more of a problem for men than for women, since we males are often taught from a very young age that "big boys" don't cry, or show emotion, or share their deepest feelings with anyone else. Boys are taught that to be emotional is to be a sissy, and because they don't want to be sissies, they learn to stuff their feelings deep down inside.

I don't want to generalize and say that most men are not capable of being truly intimate with someone. Such a statement would be absurd, of course. Nor do I want to imply that women don't have a problem in this area; of course, many do. But still, the vast majority of those who fear true intimacy and commitment are men.

True intimacy, according to Washington, NJ-pastor Mark Muncy:

- Is intensely personal (and few things that are intense are easy to develop)
- Is sustained and developed over a long period of time (it is not something that can be developed over a few dates or conversations)

- Involves self-disclosure: dropping your mask and letting the other person see who you really are (which can be frightening because it risks rejection)
- Involves accountability (it's not always easy to be held accountable for your actions)
- Involves negotiating (you can't always get your own way when you're involved in a truly intimate, give-and-take relationship) (*Pastoral Psychology* 31 (4): 1982)

Because a healthy marriage calls for lifelong intimacy, you need to know, before you marry, if you are capable of this depth of bonding with another person. It's important that you know your intended . . . but it's just as important that you know yourself. You must know, especially, if you are strong enough to complete the journey you're about to undertake.

In Luke 14, Jesus cites two examples of the importance of counting the cost before embarking on a major enterprise—in this instance, going to battle or erecting a building. Of course, what the Lord was really talking about was the cost of following Him. What Jesus is doing here is telling those who say they want to follow Him that they had better take a long, hard look at the cost involved before they head out on the road with Him. There is a heavy price to pay, and He wants to make sure that every potential disciple is aware of that.

Christ's message applies equally well to anyone who is thinking about marriage. The fact is that every year thousands of ill-prepared hopefuls float up to the altar on a cloud of romantic passion, having never considered the cost of a lifelong relationship with another human being.

They have begun the journey before they have assessed the situation to see if they really have what it takes to reach their intended destination. No wonder so many of them don't make it.

NEEDED: A MATURE ADULT IDENTITY

Some people make the mistake of marrying someone before they really know who they are. This is especially true of someone who marries very early, say right out of high school, who upon hitting age 35 or 40, suddenly begins to go through an identity crisis (or what is commonly referred to as a midlife crisis). He thinks that, well, maybe he's really some guy who ought to be driving a little red sports car and wearing a couple of heavy gold chains around his neck, rather than the guy with a station wagon, three kids, a couple of dogs, a cat, and a thick coupon book from the mortgage company.

After a year or so this person usually finds out that he really was cut out to be the guy with the station wagon, etc., but by then it's too late because he's thrown it all away.

Again, there are two important reasons why you need to have a well-developed and firm understanding of who you are before you can be truly intimate with another person.

First, identifying, understanding, and owning your thoughts and feelings will make you more capable of empathizing with others, and empathy is an important requirement of intimacy.

Second, until you identify, understand, and own your thoughts and feelings, there's no way you can possibly share them with anyone else. And sharing your innermost thoughts and secrets is part of what intimacy is all about.

I can't tell you who I am if I don't know myself.

Maybe you've heard about the plight of the poor woman who married a man for life—only to find out that he didn't have any. Yeah, you're right, that is an old joke. But it's no joke when you marry someone who has no life—who doesn't have the slightest idea of who he really is—who has no life of his own.

Do you know who you are? Have you spent time getting to know yourself? Have you examined why you feel the way you do about life in general? Do you know why you react the way you do in certain situations? Do you have an understanding of what makes you happy, sad, or angry?

If you really want to be intimate with another human being, it's not only important that you know yourself, but that you like yourself and are comfortable with who you are. In many places, the Bible talks about healthy self-love. Jesus commanded His followers to love their neighbors as much as they love themselves.

The apostle Paul directed Christians to think more highly of our brothers and sisters than we think of ourselves. But nowhere does the Bible ever tell us that we should feel bad about ourselves or put ourselves down. It's understood that we are going to see ourselves as creatures formed in the image of God, as those for whom Christ was willing to die. It's understood that a healthy man or woman is going to like and love him- or herself. It's so true that only when you love yourself are you capable of loving someone else in an intimate way, and of letting that other person love you the same way.

WHY SOME PEOPLE FEAR INTIMACY

The vulnerability that's involved in intimacy can be

highly threatening to a person who doesn't have a strong self-identity. In other words, the guy (or gal) who hasn't taken the time to figure out who he is, and why he is who he is, and who has never learned to really like himself, tends to fear emotional closeness with another human being. The reason for this usually has a lot to do with his childhood.

Specifically, there are two basic home environments that tend to produce adults who are afraid of intimacy.

In the first such home, the parents are overprotective and smothering to such a degree that the children are not allowed or encouraged to develop a healthy independence and become their own persons. In such homes it is very difficult for the child to develop a clear sense of who he is apart from his parents. He takes on his parents' values, their belief system, their approach to life, simply because he doesn't know how to do anything else.

Then, when it comes time for this child to "leave the nest" and venture out into the world, he has a very stunted image of "self." He really doesn't know who he is because the growth and maturation that should have occurred over the first eighteen to twenty years of his life has not taken place. Oftentimes, as this person begins to find his own identity emerging, he feels exhilarated, as if, for the first time in his life, he is finding out what it means to be alive. Usually, because he wants his psychological metamorphosis to continue, he is leery of entering into an intimate relationship. To him, "closeness" has always been associated with being emotionally stifled and repressed. Thus, by giving in to his most basic fears, he avoids the truest forms of intimacy. Such people frequently find themselves paying for their fear of intimacy in terms of loneliness and emotional isolation.

The second type of home which often produces adults who are afraid of intimacy is almost the exact opposite of the first. In this family, the parents tend to be emotionally distant, aloof and non-nurturing. They may do a fine job of providing for their children's physical needs, but they do not provide the emotional warmth and security every child needs to help her grow into an emotionally healthy adult. Once they reach adulthood, those who grow up in such families tend to be "clingy" and dependent on others, primarily because they are trying to make up for the love and nurturing that was denied them in their formative years.

These people don't want to be close in a healthy sense. They almost want to fuse with their partners, thus wiping out appropriate boundaries and limits. They don't know how to be truly intimate because they don't know how to respect and respond to their partner's occasional needs for space or privacy, seeing such needs as a threat to the relationship.

This person is usually very "double-minded." He wants intimacy, but he's afraid of it. His greatest fear is that he will be abandoned, and the best way to avoid that is not to get close to anyone in the first place. In most instances, though, his need is stronger than his fear and he will *have to* find someone he can cling to. Oftentimes, though, he will resent his neediness, and actually become angry at the one he needs. His attitude is, "It makes me mad to need you so much. I wish I were strong enough to stand on my own."

In this way, he's like a tiny child who wants to get dressed by himself, but can't quite do it. He becomes frustrated and angry, and when Mom comes along and tries to help him he only gets more angry and more frustrated. He doesn't want to need anybody's help . . . but he does . . . and the fact that he does drives him nuts!

Talk about being stuck between a rock and a hard place. That's what can happen if you get romantically involved with someone like this. You'll get so many mixed signals you'll start to feel like the rope at a tug-of-war. Push-pull, push-pull, push-pull. That's likely to become the story of your life!

Such people can change, but it takes a lot of work. It also takes an understanding of why they feel the way they do about themselves.

As we've discussed before, unhealthy needs can lead to unhealthy relationships. As we mentioned back in chapter 2, some of the needs that people try to fill through marriage are unhealthy—the need to escape, the need to rebel against authority, etc. If you have identified and understand your less healthy desires and motivations, it is not so likely that you will be controlled by them, and you will minimize their negative impact upon your life.

In other words, the better you understand yourself the less likely you'll be to marry someone who really isn't good for you.

Another good thing that comes from understanding yourself is the ability to understand others—to have empathy for who they are and what they are going through.

Otherwise, you may feel like folk singer Joan Baez, who, in Jill Bauer's book *From "I do" to "I'll Sue"* said, "The easiest kind of relationship for me is with ten thousand people. The hardest is with one."

But maybe you've been reading all this and thinking, "Great! Just great! All of the unhealthy examples Nicholson is using sound like excerpts from my biography! I don't really know myself. I'm out of touch with my feelings. Unhealthy needs rule my life. I might as well get out the old cyanide capsule." If that's how you're feeling, don't despair. Don't give up. Change is possible.

If this were an irreversible condition there would be a whole bunch of psychologists out of work, including me. You can bring needed changes into your life by getting to know your own personality traits, and then working to modify the ones that need to be modified.

Let's take a look at some of the four specific things you can do to gain a better understanding of your personality traits:

GETTING TO KNOW YOURSELF

Begin by writing down what you do know about your personality—or, at least, what you think you know. What do you consider to be your best qualities and attributes? What evidence tells you that you possess these traits? What do you think your negative traits are? What evidence exists for these? Don't cheat, now. Try to "step outside of yourself" and see yourself the way you really are. Don't overdo it on either the positive or negative side of the ledger. If you need to change, and want to change, you have to be honest with yourself.

Ask people who know you well to help you by drawing up a similar list about you. Promise them (and mean it) that you're not going to be angry if you read some things on their list that you don't like. You need an honest evaluation because you're looking to improve yourself. The last thing you need is flattery or false encouragement. Yes, this can be a scary thing to do. But it is worth it if you really want to change.

In fact, if you're *really* feeling brave, you might ask some folks who aren't all that crazy about you to tell you why they feel the way they do. I don't suggest this for everyone. You'd probably have to be pretty thick-skinned to do it. And you'd have to keep in mind that there are some people who will just plain not like you, and the problem may be just as likely to be theirs as it is yours. But if you're willing to listen to some negative comments about yourself, and then be strong enough to separate the nonsense from the useful information, go ahead and call that old boyfriend (or girlfriend) who broke up with you last year, who hasn't talked to you since then, and ask him to give you his honest opinion of your personality. And then, brace yourself!

If you are involved in a church, try to get one of the church leaders to help you assess your spiritual gifts. There are a number of forms, surveys, and tests that can help you in this process. An understanding of your spiritual gifts can give you a better understanding of strong areas of your personality—the ways in which God has gifted you.

Get a counselor or pastor to give you a temperament analysis instrument—such as a Taylor Johnson Temperament Analysis, a Myers-Briggs Type Indicator, or a Biblical Personal Profile System. These tests are relatively simple and inexpensive, yet they can provide interesting insights into the thought patterns and behavior that govern your life.

ARE YOU ALL GROWN UP?

Marriage isn't for children. It ought to be labeled "adults only." The only problem is that you can't tell just from looking at someone whether he's really an adult. You can be mature at eighteen or nineteen, but you can still be a kid at twenty-one, or thirty-one, or forty-one! You can be a kid even if you're six-foot-three, 240 pounds, and make a million dollars a year playing professional football. Or if you're a tall, shapely model whose photograph sells millions of calendars every year. In other words, physical maturity doesn't have anything at all to do with mental and emotional maturity.

Some people never develop what I call an MAI (Mature Adult Identity). They've never developed a sense of their own independence and competence as an adult, nor have they completely separated emotionally from their parents. The following are some questions that can help you see if you have a need for growth in this part of your life:

1. As a teenager or a young adult were you able to develop and express your own unique identity apart from your parents? If not, it is possible that you never "rebelled" against them in a healthy way. It's perfectly fine if you agree with almost everything your parents think, do, and say. But it's fine only if you've thought things through for yourself and have come to your own conclusions. It's not fine if you think and feel the way you do simply because that's the way Mom and Dad told you to think. It's really true that an unexamined opinion isn't worthy of having. One of the true marks of an adult is that he thinks for himself and makes his own decisions about things.

2. Did you ever go through a process where you intelligently examined and questioned the core beliefs and values your parents attempted to teach you?

This can be an unsettling process, that's true, but it's a necessary ingredient of developing your own identity. Ask yourself how your beliefs and values differ from those of your parents. It's not that you have to be opposed to everything they stand for, but if you don't see some differences between your beliefs and your parents' beliefs, then it's possible that you have some growing up to do.

3. Was there ever a time when you established financial independence from your parents? Have you proved yourself capable of meeting your own basic financial and material needs?

A friend of mine who got married while he and his wife were both still in college tells me how embarrassed he gets when he thinks back to the time when he decided to get married. In order to prove to both sets of parents that they were capable of making it on their own, the couple sat down and drew up a monthly household budget. They met with their parents, showing them that they had thought things through, and that they knew what it would take to make a go of things financially.

When he thinks about that now he shakes his head and says, "I don't know how our parents kept from laughing when they saw that budget. We really didn't have any idea how much things cost. We didn't know how much it cost to pay for utilities or groceries or to keep gas in the car. We'd never really been on our own . . . and we were extremely idealistic to say the least.

"We figured that twenty dollars a week for groceries was

probably plenty, and I think we budgeted about twenty or thirty dollars a month for all the utilities."

Nevertheless, this couple did marry, and were able to make a go of it, although it wasn't easy.

"There were weeks when we couldn't afford to eat anything but soup, and we both sloshed when we walked around."

Although their marriage worked out, that's not usually the case with two people who really don't know what it's like to try to make it financially out there in the "real world." The hardest year of any marriage is often the first, and one of the factors that causes the most trouble is almost always financial pressures and problems. That can be true even with two people who have been making their own way in the world for some time. You can imagine how tough it is for two people who have *never* had to pay their own way.

So, if you are thinking seriously about marriage, it is important that you first live for a time without your parents' financial help, providing your own needs, and not turning to your folks every time you get yourself in a tight spot.

4. Was there ever a time in your life when you lived on your own without significant direct emotional support from your parents?

Have you proven to yourself that you are capable of enjoying life and feeling at ease, safe and secure without direct or indirect contact with your parents for periods of up to a month? People who never get this opportunity, or who move in with a partner or spouse directly upon leaving home may not be capable of surviving in this world without having to have someone else's constant emotional support or presence. In other words, they may not be capable of the intimacy and the give-and-take that a healthy marriage requires.

Way back in 1971, Carly Simon had a hit record called "That's the Way I've Always Heard It Should Be." In the poignant lyrics of this song, she describes her parents' marriage, where her mother "sits at night with no lights on," and her father "reads his magazine." She doesn't want this type of loveless marriage for herself, and so, even though her boyfriend has asked her to marry him, she protests that if she does that now, "I'll never learn to be just me first, by myself " (Maya Productions Ltd. and Quackenbush Music Ltd., 1971). There's some wise thinking in that old record. You'd better learn to be just you first, by yourself, before you commit your life to someone else.

I once talked to a man who was brokenhearted because he had terminated a relationship with a young woman even though he cared deeply for her. He had broken up with her because every time anything the least bit troubling or unsettling came up she picked up the telephone and placed a long-distance call to her mother. It wasn't just major things that prompted that long-distance call. If they had a minor argument about something, she called her mother. If she had an upset stomach she called her mother for advice. If she accidentally bounced a check, or had a toothache, or burned a roast or . . . well, almost anything was likely to precipitate a call to her mother. In fact, she called her mother every day, and it was apparent that she just couldn't function without her mother's emotional support and guidance. She was not ready to make it on her own, and she was most certainly not ready for marriage. The end result was that her boyfriend decided to terminate the relationship. It was probably the wisest thing he could have done.

5. When you interact with your parents now, can you approach them on an adult-to-adult basis?

Is there still a part of you that is afraid to confront them when you think they are wrong or when they have offended you? Are you able to express anger toward your parents in an appropriate manner without feeling guilty about it? Is there still a part of you that is trying to gain the approval and praise from your parents that you feel they always withheld from you during your growing-up years?

Going back through the five questions we've asked, if you answered "no" to most of them, it's possible that you still feel like a child when you're dealing with your parents. What can you do about it? You can start appropriately but firmly asserting yourself with them.

This may mean something as simple as expressing a reasoned dissenting opinion on a certain topic. It may also involve something as complex and involved as appropriately confronting them regarding past hurts and grievances. But before you take this last step, consider consulting a pastor, a counselor, or a trusted friend to get their feedback on what you plan to say and how you plan to say it. If you handle such a confrontation hastily or in an inappropriate manner, you'll wind up doing much more harm than good.

Nevertheless, there are times when confrontation is absolutely necessary.

The Bible describes marriage this way: "A man shall leave his father and mother and be joined to his wife, and they shall become one flesh" (Gen. 2:24); and, "So . . . they are no longer two but one flesh" (Matt. 19:6).

This is the sort of intimacy that is required in a marriage relationship. The husband must put his wife first and the wife must put her husband first. No other relationship should ever be allowed over the marital relationship or to impact it in a negative way. Are you ready for that kind of an arrangement? Are you ready to give yourself to your loved one in that deep, committed fashion?

Are you capable of being truly intimate? If you're considering marriage, that's a very important question—one that can't remain unanswered.

Eight

Is That a Monkey in Your Family Tree?

Do you come from a dysfunctional family?

If so . . . welcome to the club.

I know that sounds kind of flippant, but the truth is that almost everybody these days seems to think his or her family of origin was (or is) dysfunctional in some ways. If you look back on your growing-up years as negative or harmful to you, then you may be wondering how your family background may influence your hopes and plans for your future, and specifically for your own future marriage and your own family. Or you may be dating or even engaged to someone who had a negative family background, and wondering what effect that will have on him or her.

When you get right down to it, it's probably true, to some degree, that we all come from dysfunctional families. After all, it's been nearly 2,000 years since this planet of ours has seen the presence of a perfect human being. All of the other men and women who have walked this earth have been flawed in some way, and that means there haven't been any perfect parents, or perfect children, or perfect brothers and sisters—which means, in turn, that there haven't been any perfect families.

Still, my opinion is that there are a lot of people blaming their parents for things that aren't really Mom and Dad's fault at all, and an awful lot of people thinking they came from "terribly dysfunctional families," when the truth is that they came from families where some of the goings-on may have been just a little bit "off-center," but then who didn't? The question is, were you harmed by the family in which you grew up? Are you carrying around baggage that needs to be dealt with before you can enter into a healthy romantic relationship with another human being? And then, once you've examined *your* family of origin, we come to a question that is just as important: What about your *loved one's* family of origin?

You've got to be mighty careful if you find some monkeys climbing around in that family tree!

Now, I like to look on the positive side of things. I think it's wise to focus on the good things of life, while acknowledging but not concentrating on the bad. I've known people, as I'm sure you have, who go around seeking to blame their parents for everything that's wrong with them, or for every mistake they've made in life. They say, "Well, it's not my fault that I have such trouble telling the truth. You know my mother was a terrible liar." Or,

"I've really tried to be faithful, but my dad had a roving eye, and I guess I just learned it from my father."

I'm sure that many relatively innocent parents are being dumped on for things they never did—and that's a shame. But even if they did make some serious mistakes, for their adult children to absolve themselves of any responsibility for having retained these same negative behavior patterns is, well . . . irresponsible.

However, and it is a big however, there are also many parents who didn't have the slightest idea of how to raise children, and who made a terrible mess of things. There are parents who were addicted to alcohol or drugs, who were abusive and violent, who were cold and indifferent, who were smothering and overprotective, who were ignorant, fearful, and prejudiced, and who hammered those same feelings into their offspring.

There are parents who never, for a single day of their lives, modeled for their children what a good relationship between a man and a woman should be like. And, as a result of the harm some of these people have inflicted upon their children, those children have grown up to be dysfunctional adults. Some of them can't hold down a job, or make friends, or relate to the world in a rational way. Many of them are unable to form healthy romantic relationships with members of the opposite sex.

But one thing I want you to remember is that it really doesn't matter how bad your parents might have been. You are not required to live your life chained to the past. Whatever your parents—or any other family members—may have done that scarred you, you can work to overcome it and get on with living a more positive, fulfilling life.

In other words, evolution *is* possible. In other words,

just because your parents might be monkeys, that doesn't mean *you* have to remain one! (This is a metaphor, folks. I'm not trying to restart the creation versus evolution debate.)

How will you be able to reach the stars if you come from a dysfunctional family full of people who tend to remind you of, well . . . dare I say it? Baboons.

You have to start by coming to an understanding of the ways in which your family has affected you. If there are wounds that need to heal and hang-ups that must be overcome, you need to know what it was that caused those wounds and those hang-ups in the first place. You may be saying, "Well, that makes sense! Why is Nicholson making such a big deal out of this?"

Because it is not always easy to confront your past in a healthy and constructive way. It's one thing to say, "Oh, my parents really messed me up," or even to say, "Hey, I had the best mom and dad anyone ever had." It's quite another thing to take a long, hard look at some parts of your life that might be painful to remember.

I will always remember one seventeen-year-old girl, an eleventh grader who would have been pretty but for her shaved head. She told me very matter-of-factly that she hated her family. There wasn't any venom in her words, and no deep anger. She might as well have been saying, "Nice weather we're having isn't it?" But her words were, "I hate my family."

She had just finished explaining to me why she was failing all of her classes in school and why she had become a regular abuser of alcohol, marijuana, and speed. Nothing really mattered to her except the hatred she felt for her mother and sisters—and her father, who had skipped out when she was twelve. It was going to take many counseling sessions before we were able to deal with that hatred and begin to put her family and her life back together.

A few days earlier a good friend of mine, a woman more than twenty years older than my teenage client, had expressed similar feelings toward her family after returning home from a visit over the Thanksgiving holidays.

"I was hoping," she told me, "that it was going to be different this time." But, of course, it hadn't been different. It had been the same old horror story. For nearly forty years she had been victimized by interpersonal patterns that made her crazy, and also made her thankful that she lived several hundred miles away from her aging parents.

"Once or twice a year," she told me, "is more than often enough to see them."

I see and hear enough of this type of thing that I am sometimes tempted to think that "the happy family" is a Hollywood fiction, or something invented by Madison Avenue as an advertising gimmick. In its more extreme, "We have no serious conflicts" form, it is a myth. Every family has problems, and at times those problems become quite serious.

Yet I know the mostly happy, mostly stable family exists. I know because I am fortunate enough to have come from one.

I love my parents. They were great to me, although I didn't always know they were being great to me. I know I could do a lot worse than to model my behavior as a parent after my mother and father, or my behavior as a husband after my father. I am grateful for my parents' influence in my life and the many things I have learned from them.

But what about you? What are the things you have

learned from your parents? Are they mostly negative, hurtful things, or mostly positive? Are you one of those who thinks, "The last thing I ever want is a marriage like the one my parents had"?

HISTORY DOESN'T HAVE TO REPEAT ITSELF

Remember that unless you make a conscious effort to do otherwise, you will tend to repeat the patterns—both positive and negative—of your parents.

Once again, if you have a pen handy, get it out and underline that last paragraph. It's one of the most important things I could tell you, and it's something that we'll keep coming back to as we talk about your plans for marital and familial happiness.

If an adult child from a dysfunctional family is not aware of his family's negative dynamics, he will tend to repeat those same patterns within his own family. Overreaction can be a problem, too. In other words, sometimes an adult child who has come out of a dysfunctional family will react so strongly against his parents' behavior that he'll go too far the other way with his own children, with the result that his family is just as dysfunctional as the family he grew up in—only in a wholly different way. For example, a woman whose own mother was distant and cold may be so overly protective and so overly involved in her children's lives that she drives them away from her. She's left sad and alone and wondering why her children could be so ungrateful when she has done everything for them that she wanted her mother to do for her. She fails to see that she has overcorrected the problem and created a situation that has been just as painful and hard to handle for her children as her own childhood was for her.

Another example might be a man whose father was overly strict and abusive so that he in turn refuses to discipline his children at all, letting them run wild and indulge in totally irresponsible behavior.

Still, the more likely result of a childhood spent in a dysfunctional family is that those dysfunctional patterns will be repeated. A child who grew up in an abusive environment is likely to become an abusive parent. A child who had alcoholic parents is likely to become an alcoholic himself—or to marry one. The boy who never saw his father express the slightest tender emotion toward his mother will most likely be unable to express love and tenderness toward the woman with whom he wants to spend the rest of his life. The girl whose mother was frivolous and self-indulgent won't know how to make the personal sacrifices that are necessary to make a go of a marriage.

History tends to repeat itself.

The files from any Child Protective Services office can yield the clearest, strongest, saddest, and most puzzling examples of this principle. It is a documented fact that many of the worst perpetrators of emotional, physical, and sexual abuse upon children were abused in similar fashion during their childhoods. Why would anyone who knows firsthand the horrific consequences of what they are about to do go ahead and inflict torture on an innocent child? The answer to this question is well beyond the scope of this book . . . but these examples serve as evidence of the powerful and lasting influence a negative childhood can have on someone's life.

BUT WE'RE JUST A LITTLE BIT DYSFUNCTIONAL

Hopefully, you didn't grow up in a home where there was abuse, where one or both of your parents was an alcoholic, or where your parents were distant and dispassionate. But there are problems that can arise out of seemingly "ordinary" families, too. For example:

- A father passes to his son the idea that "real men" don't show their feelings. When that son becomes a father he is non-expressive and non-nurturing, so his children do not feel that he loves them.
- A mother sets her daughter up for marital failure by teaching her from the time she is young that sex is a necessary evil, something to be tolerated but never enjoyed.
- A workaholic repeats his father's example and injures his children's self-esteem by his absence: missing every important event of their lives due to his "having to work."
- A woman who is angry at men in general because of her sadness and resentment over never feeling loved and appreciated by her father teaches her daughters—and her sons, too—that men cannot be trusted. As a result, none of her daughters are ever capable of establishing a close, caring relationship with a man. Her sons live up to her expectations by becoming the kind of men who can't be trusted—at least not by women. (Or the boys may grow up to be ashamed of and troubled by their own masculinity.)
- A man who orders his wife around as if she were more

his slave than his partner will instill in his sons the belief that women are inferior to men and thus deserve such treatment. Chances are that this man is acting out the things he learned from watching his father's behavior, and that his sons will perpetuate this misogynistic and abusive behavior to the third generation.

- A wife cannot "fight fair" because she never observed a healthy argument in her home when she was a child. She doesn't know how to express herself without becoming angry and abusive, and she doesn't know how to open up and listen to what her partner is saying. In extreme cases, children either saw abusive anger spewed forth in the form of verbal poison or they saw tight smiles hiding unresolved bitterness.

The Bible tells us that the sins of the fathers may be visited upon the children for several generations (Ex. 20:5). In situations like the ones we've been discussing, this is most definitely true. Some of these negative, harmful behavior patterns have been carried out in families for generation after generation. A father who abuses his wife raises a son who abuses his wife who raises a son who abuses his wife . . . and so on. But the good news is that the patterns don't *have* to be repeated. We are creatures of free will, and that means we can decide not to perpetuate these "sins" of our mothers and fathers, that we can choose right now to take steps to break the cycle of dysfunctional behavior.

The biggest and hardest step is usually the first, which is acknowledging that there is a problem that needs to be overcome. Alcoholics Anonymous has had a great deal of success with its 12-Step Program over the years, and the first step for the person who wants help is to admit that he has a problem and it holds him in its grip. Over the last several years these twelve steps have been modified and are used by churches and other organizations to help people who are struggling against addictions and dysfunctional behaviors of all kinds. In each of these situations, the first step remains the same—admission of the problem.

Once you've made that admission, you can begin to fight the problem. You can make decisions and engage in behavior patterns that are contrary to your "normal" way of functioning, and you can thereby break free from whatever binds you. You can also strive to resolve the conflicts and hurts that have brought about the problem in the first place.

For example, suppose that when you were a child, one or both of your parents were dominating and controlling. As a result, you now blow up in anger whenever anyone asks or tells you to do anything. Even the slightest suggestions cause you to feel the old angers and tensions rising inside. Well, you know this attitude isn't going to make you one of the most popular people in town, and it certainly isn't going to work well within the give-and-take arena of a marriage. What are you going to do?

You could start by confronting, as lovingly as possible, your controlling and demanding parents. You need to discuss past grievances—tell them how their controlling of your life has hurt you—and then strive as hard as you possibly can to be appropriately assertive in your current dealings with them.

I know it won't be a piece of cake. It can be a very difficult thing to do, but it can also be a very worthwhile thing to do.

But what if you just can't bring yourself to confront your parents?

Then start by writing a letter. I'm not suggesting that you should pour out all of your anger in that letter. Everything should be done with as much love as you can possibly muster. But if you can't bring yourself to speak face-to-face to someone who has hurt you and left you struggling for wholeness, then writing a letter can be a good place to start.

Another question: What if my parents won't listen to me?

That's a possibility. But you will have the satisfaction of knowing that you have done everything you can do to explain yourself to them. If they refuse to listen and change, you must still resolve that you will not let them control you any longer.

What if your parents are dead?

If that's the case, it can still be cleansing and helpful to write a letter to them, explaining the ways in which they hurt you. Pray about the situation, and ask God to help you to obtain peace and freedom regarding your parents' role in your life. And you can get help by discussing the situation with a professional therapist.

Once you have dealt with this problem in as thorough a manner as possible, you will be less likely to overreact to normal requests on the part of your future spouse—and that's the type of thing that can help to keep you out of divorce court.

OUCH! THAT HURTS!

Have you ever touched someone on the back or shoulder and had them practically jump out of their skin?

"Ow—hey, don't touch me there! That hurts!"

"Oh, I'm sorry, I didn't mean to hurt you."

"That's okay. It's just that I spent the weekend at the beach—and I've got *such* a bad sunburn!"

Well, of course, if you knew the person was in pain from a sunburn, you wouldn't have touched him. But you had no way of knowing.

That's the way it is with these emotional hurts that we carry around because of hurts from years ago. Other people don't see them, so they may accidentally touch those painful areas every once in awhile. When they do, they might have to get out the big spatula and scrape us off the ceiling.

"Hey, what made him go off on me like that?"

"I don't know. You must have hit a nerve!"

"But how? What'd I do?"

Sometimes, people may be genuinely mystified and surprised by what they see as overreaction to a simple remark and well-intentioned action.

Sometimes a person may have carried around that "sore spot" for so long that he's come to think of it as normal. This person may assume that everyone has the same sore areas and responds in the same way to being touched in those areas. He doesn't understand why the recipient of his anger is so surprised by it, because, after all, "Wouldn't everybody react the same way in the same situation?"

You can see why it is so important that these emotional injuries be healed. Once you have obtained healing, you can interact with people—including the ones you love the most—in all sorts of ways that never were possible before, because they used to hurt so much. Healing may also bring with it renewed energy and vigor, primarily because you no longer have to invest so much emotional energy in such activities as harboring grudges, nursing resentments, repressing old hurts, or feeling sorry for yourself.

Let's look briefly at some of the ways your parents may have "damaged" you, and talk about how to overcome them.

You may have been overprotected and pampered as a child, so you may expect your boyfriend or girlfriend to take care of you in the same way dear old Mumsy and Daddy did. Parental overindulgence can cause difficulty in two ways. First, it can lead to an adult who thinks he *deserves* to be spoiled and pampered. Second, it can lead to an adult who thinks someone else *has* to do all sorts of things for him because he's too weak and helpless to do them for himself. Either way, you can begin to overcome this problem by acknowledging your previously pampered position as being unhealthy, and working to develop more realistic expectations of your needs and the needs of your romantic partner.

Your parents may have been distant and unloving, so you may have a hunger for love that has made you clingy, possessive, and overly demanding of your partner's attention. If you fail to understand and confront your reasons for feeling this way, you will probably be continually frustrated by your partner's reaction to you. And, too, you will exasperate your partner because he or she will never be able to give you enough loving attention.

Appropriately confronting your parents can help to reduce your anger toward them—anger that has been transferred to your partner. It can also help you begin the process of grieving for the childhood you never had which, in turn, can help you accept your current situation and will increase the likelihood that you will be content with the attention and affection your loved one is able to give you.

If you are a woman who was sexually abused during your formative years, you may have trouble trusting men, and that means, of course, that it's going to be very difficult for you to form a loving, intimate relationship with a husband. You may also feel that a healthy sexual relationship is out of the question. But intensive involvement in therapy that involves some direct or symbolic confrontation with the one who abused you can help you feel more empowered and can increase the likelihood that you will be able to form a trusting and sexually fulfilling relationship with your future husband.

Perhaps you grew up in a home where the abuse was more subtle. It was not sexual, or physical, but it was there just the same, in the form of verbal abuse . . . words like "stupid," and "helpless" and "worthless" that were spit at you whenever you did the least little thing wrong. The adult who grew up in this kind of environment is likely to suppress his anger in an unhealthy way, and to want those around him to do the same. Over time, this can lead to bitterness, physical problems, and emotional distance between family members. But by accepting anger as a legitimate emotion, and by working on expressing it in an appropriate way, you can learn to overcome your fear of anger, and learn to use it as an effective part of your "coping" mechanism.

It's important to know your vulnerable areas, and to understand the ways in which your childhood experiences helped to bring them about. Having this knowledge can help you reach a more settled understanding of who you are and where you have come from. Confronting and resolving these childhood "injuries" is the only way you can get free of them. That is the only way you can make peace with your past, and see that the cycle of pain and dysfunctional behavior begins to stop *right now!*

Nine

Marriage: Straight from the Heart of God

One man and one woman, committed to each other for life. That has always been God's design for marriage, beginning in the Garden of Eden when He put Adam and Eve together.

Unfortunately, right from the start, man began messing around with God's plan, trying to improve on it. Before this planet was more than a few hundred years old, men had decided that one wife wasn't enough. Instead of the one-to-one partnership that was designed by God, they began treating their wives as possessions instead of partners. Because men, in general, were physically stronger than women, it was fairly easy for them to dominate and control the females of the species, and so that's what they did.

It wasn't uncommon for a man to have three or four wives or even more—and that was never the way God had intended it to be.

Unfortunately, that's still the way it is today for many people. The only difference is that they have only one wife or one husband at a time, but they still have many partners within the course of a lifetime. And that's not God's best for humankind.

Running for the divorce court every time you feel dissatisfied with your partner is not the way to fulfill the divine goals, objectives, and spiritual potential for which marriage is intended. I believe that many married couples struggle because they have never understood God's purpose for marriage nor the power He offers to keep a marriage working properly. So let's spend some time taking a look at God's purposes for marriage.

A few years ago I attended a weekend seminar called the FamilyLife Marriage Conference, which offered a great presentation of God's biblical blueprints for marriage. Most of the concepts in this chapter are adapted from this material with the permission of FamilyLife. (For more information on FamilyLife Marriage Conferences see Appendix A.)

TO REPRODUCE GODLY CHILDREN

On two occasions God has commanded His people to be fruitful and multiply—in other words, to have children. He gave that order to Adam and Eve in the Garden of Eden and He repeated it to Noah's family after the Great Flood had destroyed all other life on this planet.

God created men and women to be His representatives, beings who would glorify Him on earth by living their lives according to His will. Through the raising up of a line of godly descendants, God's representation on earth would increase, and thus, so would His influence. This influence would help to thwart the plans and purposes of Satan.

A healthy marriage involving a oneness between a husband and wife is necessary in order to raise godly children. As a practical matter before you get married, ask yourself if your beloved is someone with whom you can raise a godly family. Does he care about God? Is there an understanding of the importance of spiritual matters? The Bible warns Christians that there is a danger that comes from being "unequally yoked" with unbelievers (2 Cor. 6:14), and this is especially true when it comes to marriage.

TO MANAGE GOD'S CREATION

When God created the first man, He placed him in the Garden of Eden and gave him the job of tending and dressing all the plants and trees there. Genesis 2:15 says, "Then the LORD God took the man and put him in the garden of Eden to tend and keep it." Then, when He saw that the man was lonely, and that he needed a helper, He created the first woman.

God told this first man and woman to "fill the earth and subdue it; have dominion over the fish of the sea, over the birds of the air, and over every living thing that moves on the earth" (Gen. 1:28).

God wants us, as His people, to be in control of life

instead of the other way around. He doesn't want us to be drifting along with the tide, just going with the flow.

A healthy marriage characterized by a sense of oneness and unity is necessary in order to maintain control over all the different aspects and variables of life. A husband and wife should support each other and encourage each other as they both strive to fulfill God's destiny for their lives.

TO MUTUALLY COMPLETE ONE ANOTHER

1 Corinthians 11:11 says, "Neither is man independent of woman, nor woman independent of man."

And in Genesis 2:18, we find God saying, "It is not good that man should be alone; I will make him a helper comparable to him."

In a marriage the way God has designed it to be, there is a completeness that is brought about through the union of two human beings that is not there when either one of them is by himself or herself.

It is not a matter of "I am insufficient by myself." It is, instead, a matter of, "My life is so much fuller and richer because you are a part of it. I could do okay by myself, but I do so much better because I'm with you!"

God knew that every one of us could use a little help to reach his or her full potential—and He isn't the only One who knows that!

The truth is that men and women *in general* need each other, and this is true on the individual level as well. God's purpose for marriage is that one man and one woman should find their mutual completeness and fulfillment in each other. God intends couples to share life with each other, in essence to drive each other out of themselves and into a wider area of contact with life.

A good question to ask yourself is whether your intended partner has a personality that complements your own. Do you fill each other's gaps? Will there be a completeness in your togetherness that is not there when you are alone?

TO REPLACE ISOLATION WITH COMPANIONSHIP

"And the LORD God said, 'It is not good that man should be alone'" (Gen. 2:18).

I don't know about you, but it touches me when I think about God, looking down on Adam in the Garden of Eden, and thinking, "Adam is lonely. He needs a friend. He needs someone he can love . . . someone to love him back."

Now, you know, Adam wasn't *really* alone in the Garden of Eden. After all, he had a close, wonderful relationship with God Himself. But for whatever reason, God decided that even *that* wasn't really enough. Adam needed his God, certainly, but he needed something more, too. He needed a relationship with a creature who was on his own level. He needed a close, intimate relationship with someone he could relate to as an equal and a partner.

And so God, in all His wisdom, created the first woman and presented her to Adam.

And how did Adam react?

I like the way *The Living Bible* puts it:

"This is it!" Adam exclaimed (Gen. 2:23 TLB).

Can't you just hear the exuberance in Adam's voice? He took one look at Eve and he was totally blown away. (Of course, she was naked at the time, so that helped.) I'm sure he thought, "Yes! My lonely days are over!"

And they were.

In those early days of creation, almost everything was perfect in this world. There was only one thing that wasn't right, and that was that there was one unpleasant emotion: loneliness.

You see, God created human beings in such a way that we need others. We need them to help us reach our full potential and to experience optimal fulfillment.

How tragic it is, and has always been—to be alone.

But if you are contemplating marriage, here's an important question to ask: Will you truly find companionship with the person you're planning to marry? Could this be the person you'd enjoy just sitting and talking to? Are you really comfortable talking to this person? Can you sit in silence with this person and still feel that you are not alone?

Remember that the majority of life is not spent at the theater, at parties, or even making love. The bulk of life consists of doing simple, mundane things and thus, if you don't feel comfortable simply "being with" and talking to another person, your marriage is likely to be a difficult one.

TO MODEL CHRIST'S RELATIONSHIP WITH THE CHURCH

" 'For this reason a man shall leave his father and mother and be joined to his wife, and the two shall become one flesh.' This is a great mystery, but I speak concerning Christ and the church" (Eph. 5:31–32).

She sat in my office with tears streaming down her face.

"I just don't want to be married to him anymore," she

sobbed. "I know how the Lord feels about divorce, but I just don't think I can take it anymore."

She stopped for a moment, trying to capture her composure. She dabbed at her eyes with a Kleenex, sniffed back some tears, and then went on. By now, her big blue eyes, which were normally clear and bright, were cloudy, and seemed to be swimming in a sea of red.

"He wants to know where every penny goes. If I spend as much as one dollar on myself, he throws a fit.

"And sex . . ." she shook her head. "He used to be so romantic, so loving and tender. Now, he's more like a caveman. Whenever he's ready, he's ready, and he expects me to be ready, too. If I'm not, he sulks. If I don't feel well . . . it doesn't matter."

Once again, the tears began to flow.

This lovely lady wasn't married to a brawler or a drinker. He wasn't some Neanderthal who didn't know any better than to treat his wife that way. Certainly, the situation would have been a tragedy no matter what.

But this man was a churchgoing Christian! In fact, he was on the church board—served as a deacon, and headed several church committees.

But according to what I was hearing from his sobbing wife, he had no understanding of God's plan and purpose for marriage.

You see, marriage is an illustration and a practical example of a deep spiritual truth—the relationship of Christ our Savior to His bride, the church. The reverse is true, too. By that, I mean that the relationship of Christ to His church can also be used as a practical example for how husbands and wives should interact with each other on a day-to-day basis. As Les Carter writes in his book, *The Push-Pull Marriage* (Grand Rapids: Baker Book House, 1983), "Marriage symbolizes the union between God and man—it manifests in a tangible human experience the love of God."

Oneness within the marriage relationship is necessary in order to accurately model the relationship between Christ and His church. When people who say they are followers of Christ conduct their marriages in unhealthy and dysfunctional ways, God's reputation is affected. Christian marriage was intended to mirror through the husband how Christ unconditionally loves, leads, and serves His church.

I'm sure you know that one of the Ten Commandments is "You shall not take the name of the LORD your God in vain" (Ex. 20:7). I don't know about you, but I was always taught that what this meant was that you didn't use the name of the Lord for a swear word. And, yes, that's certainly part of the meaning of this commandment. But there's more to it than that. We are also guilty of taking His name in vain if we say we belong to Him—that is, if we call ourselves Christians—and then live in blatant disregard of His laws and His teachings.

This is true of every aspect of our lives, but especially within the marriage relationship. God's plan for marriage calls for love, respect, and tenderness on a daily basis. It calls for overlooking the little irritations, and for focusing instead on the positive, for loving your wife or your husband as much as you love and cherish your own body. God's plan for marriage calls for the living out of the definition of love as contained in the 13th chapter of 1 Corinthians.

In a Christian marriage, the husband is commanded to

love his wife in the same way Christ loves His church. And Christ loves the church so much that He was willing to suffer and die for her, so much that He intercedes for her on a daily basis, so much that He sees her only as beautiful and righteous and virtuous no matter what her past life has been like.

In a Christian marriage, the wife is commanded to reverently subject herself to her husband's authority as the church willingly yields to the authority and leadership of Christ.

Both roles must be properly fulfilled to demonstrate Christ's relationship with the church. When Christians fail to model a godly relationship in marriage, non-Christians get a warped perspective of God's ideal.

Understanding all of these spiritual dimensions of marriage can help us understand why a healthy Christian marriage is such an important matter to God, and why He states with such emphasis, "I hate divorce" (Mal. 2:16 NIV).

As a practical thought, ask yourself if the person you're planning to marry has the spiritual understanding that will be required to help the two of you model Christ's relationship with the church.

If not, some rethinking may be in order.

THE WORLD'S VIEW OF MARRIAGE

Now that we've taken a look at marriage from a godly perspective, let's turn things around and look at some of the human misperceptions about the matrimonial state. We human beings tend to believe that marriage is for:

- personal fulfillment
- procreation

- meeting the other person half way

Let me explain how these views differ from the way God looks at marriage.

First, if you look at marriage as a means of personal fulfillment, then you're perfectly free to walk away from it if it isn't making you happy. At the first sign of trouble—the first time your wife burns dinner or the first time your husband tracks footprints onto your freshly waxed floor—you can pack up your things and head back home to Mom and Dad.

How many times has Elizabeth Taylor been married? Seven? Eight? She's been married to more people than some of us have even dated. She's been married to more people than some of us even *know*! Do you suppose that she tends to view marriage as something to be discarded when it's not making her happy and satisfied? I have a feeling that's the case. But I'm not singling her out, because if that truly is Elizabeth Taylor's attitude, it's an attitude that reflects the society in which she lives.

As I've said before, everyone is selfish to some degree, and we all tend to have the attitude that asks, "What's in it for me?" But marriage is not a matter of getting something for yourself. It's a matter of giving to someone else. It is a loving commitment that is to endure "for better or for worse, in sickness and in health."

Marriage can be hard. It takes tremendous effort to make it work. But it is one of God's greatest gifts to mankind, and it is worth every bit of effort we put into it.

The second way in which the human view of marriage differs from God's view is that we tend to see it as a means of procreation, of propagating the human race.

While this is closely tied in with God's view, there is one difference. As we have discussed, in God's eyes marriage is meant to produce *godly* children. Not just children, but *godly* children.

It's possible for just about any healthy man and woman to become parents. The birth of a child is the natural result of the sexual union between a man and a woman. But that's where the work starts. That's where the process of teaching, training, and inculcating godly values into your child begins. God's Word says, "Train up a child in the way he should go, and when he is old he will not depart from it" (Prov. 22:6).

In the first chapter of 2 Timothy, the apostle Paul writes to his young friend, "I thank God . . . when I call to remembrance the genuine faith that is in you, which dwelt first in your grandmother Lois and your mother Eunice, and I am persuaded is in you also" (vv. 3–5). It was no accident that Timothy became one of the great leaders in the church of the first century. He learned about God from his mother and his grandmother. He had a godly heritage, and that was reflected in the man he became.

It is so important that your future children receive godly instruction and guidance. It's not enough to think that they will be okay simply because you love them. Nor is it enough to think that they will grow up to be good Christians because (after all) they are your children. They will need you to read Bible stories to them. They will need you to see to it that they attend Sunday school and church. They will need you to pray with them and teach them how to develop a one-on-one relationship with God through Christ.

All of these things are so important—especially in this

day when evil seems to be gaining the upper hand throughout much of society.

The third way in which we tend to have a different (and thus wrong) perspective about marriage is that we believe it is a fifty-fifty proposition, a relationship in which we can meet our partner halfway and expect him or her, in turn, to meet *us* halfway.

But instead, God's intention for marriage is that both partners be willing to give one hundred percent of themselves to meet the other person's needs. It is to be as it is in *The Gift of the Magi* by O'Henry (New York: Franklin Watts, 1967), in which neither the husband nor wife can possibly do enough for each other, in which each feels compelled to demonstrate their love for the other.

Does that sound idealistic?

It's what God wants from His people.

You see, part of the problem is that it's very hard to know when you're meeting someone halfway.

Have you ever played "telephone," that game where you whisper something to the first person in line, who whispers it to the next person, and so on? When the message gets to the end of the line, the first person in line explains out loud what he said, and the last person has to say what he heard. Almost always, the original statement has become twisted and distorted so that it's unrecognizable. Why? Because of misperceptions and misunderstandings.

Have you read two reviews of a book or movie and found that the critics completely disagreed? That happens because different people see things in different ways.

Have you ever carpooled with anyone? If you have, you know how hard it can be to keep things straight: "Let's see,

I drove Tuesday and Wednesday, so you need to drive Thursday and Friday."

"But wait a minute. I drove Monday, Tuesday, *and* Wednesday the week before, and . . ."

Because of human nature, it's not unusual, in a situation like that, for both parties to think they're doing more than their share of the driving, and that the other person is getting off easy.

My point is that we tend to see the things we do for other people as great mountains and the things they do for us as insignificant hills. But the truth is that if you think you're doing everything you can possibly do to meet the other person's needs, you're probably doing enough to meet him halfway.

A marriage or any type of relationship is in trouble if one or both of the partners thinks, "If you do your part, I'll do mine." In this situation, acceptance is based upon performance and giving is based upon the other person being deserving. But love and giving within a marriage should be unconditional, given not because the other person deserves it, but because you love them so much and have committed your life to them.

There are some other problems here, too. First of all, a fifty-fifty split is not always possible. Because of an illness, or job loss, or some other negative situation, people are frequently unable to pull an exact half of the load, and it may be unrealistic and unfair to expect them to do so.

Also, your love may be doing more on behalf of the relationship than you know. All of the things the other person does may not be immediately apparent, just as all the things you do are not immediately apparent, either.

But that's all right, as long as you're doing them out of love, and not because you want to be appreciated.

THE SEARCH FOR TRUE INTIMACY

Let's take the time to briefly recap some of the important points we've covered in this book. I hope that by now you:

1. Understand which are healthy and which are unhealthy reasons for getting married
2. Can debunk the lies some believe in regard to love, engagement, or marriage
3. Understand and appreciate the elements that go into the development of a healthy relationship between one man and one woman
4. Grasp the healthy and unhealthy aspects of the mate-selection process
5. Know the importance of learning how to communicate well, and of confronting and resolving conflicts as soon as possible rather than allowing things to build up and fester
6. Understand what it means to achieve true intimacy in marriage
7. Acknowledge and can start to overcome factors in your upbringing that will hinder your relationship with your future spouse
8. See marriage the way God sees it

But even if you became a walking encyclopedia of *every* fact about marriage known to man, even if you were able to comprehensively address and resolve every premarital issue ever considered by the best premarital counselor in the history of the world, even if you came to understand the spiritual purposes of marriage better than the apostle Paul himself, even if you did all of those things, you would still never be able to get all your needs for deepest intimacy met through your mate.

Uh, oh. I can hear you now.

"What are you talking about? You took us through all of these steps and now you're saying, 'It doesn't work'?"

No, that's not what I'm saying.

What I *am* saying is that there is an intimacy that goes deeper than the marriage relationship, and if you are missing out on that then you are *really* missing out! Henri Nouwen, the noted theologian and writer explains it this way:

> I come together with others . . . out of the recognition that they belong to the same heart I belong to, and that they cannot fulfill the deepest yearnings of my heart. Why? Because God has created in me a heart that can only be satisfied by the One who created it. God has given me a heart that yearns to be loved so much and so intimately that only the One who has given me that heart can give that love. And it is only there in God that I can basically trust that I am well held *(Alive Now! Nov./Dec. 1991).*

You see, God has created the human heart in such a way that we crave to be loved with an intensity and completeness that no human being can ever fully deliver. What Dr. Nouwen is saying is that it is only through a relationship with God that a human being can get his deepest intimacy needs fully met.

So please focus on the steps to a healthy relationship we have discussed in this book. But also be sure to nourish your relationship with the living God who created you and who desires His best for you and all your relationships.

Appendix A

COMMUNICATION IS VITAL

Listen to this story from Jill Bauer's book *From "I Do" to "I'll Sue"*: "Rodney Chavez, estranged from his wife, Brenda, invited her to his home, then handcuffed her, 'hog-tied' her by tying her ankles to her wrists, and according to a police officer, 'tried to get her to reconcile'" (New York: Plume/Meridian, 1993).

Hmmmm. Do you think that maybe Mr. Chavez was having a bad hair day? I wonder what he did after he had Brenda all tied up like that? Did he try to give her some roses, turn the lights down low, and maybe put some Frank Sinatra records on the stereo?

Well, I guess the one thing that can be said for the fellow was that he sure didn't believe in sweet-talking her. So you think she was willing to consider reconciling? Of course not! And, while I hope that anyone who is reading this book would immediately see the error involved in that kind of behavior, I am convinced that the vast majority of us need significant improvements in our ability to communicate. We don't go around tying people's wrists and ankles together to try to get them to listen to us, but I'm afraid that sometimes we're not a lot more subtle than that.

Please don't take offense at what I just said. Believe me when I tell you that I include myself among the clumsy. I've had to work hard to learn how to communicate properly.

The truth is that proper, effective communication can be difficult. It takes practice and learning, on the part of the one communicating *and* the one being communicated to! In this appendix are information and resources that will help you polish your communication skills even further.

Communication involves the full and appropriate expression

of thoughts and feelings on the part of both partners. It involves each partner being able to listen to and empathize with the other. And, finally, it involves the ability of each partner to address and resolve conflict.

Couples who can do all those things—who can communicate effectively and resolve conflict before it has become an infection within the relationship—have a significantly better chance of making their marriage a success when compared with those who struggle with communications skills or who tend to sweep problems under the rug, hoping things will get better by themselves. If you want a happy, successful marriage, you *must* know the fine art of interpersonal communication.

That this is true has been proven by fifteen years of research undertaken by Dr. Howard Markman from the University of Denver. Dr. Markman has a communications program, PREP, that involves some lectures on various aspects of married life, but its key component is intensive training on how to communicate clearly and effectively, how to "fight" fairly, and how to overcome conflict.

Dr. Markman believes that initial compatibility between a couple is not nearly as important to an enduring partnership as is the development of proper communication skills, and statistics tend to support his belief.

His latest figures show that after twelve years, couples who participated in his program have a breakup rate that is about half of that for couples who have not had such training. In addition to that, PREP graduates were able to maintain their relationship satisfaction levels far longer than those couples who did not receive training.

Several years ago my wife Cindy and I participated in a short, three-day course, directed by Dr. Markman, Dr. Scott Stanley, and Dr. Susan Blumberg, on how to become certified PREP instructors. Thus, I can attest to the fact that he and his associates have developed a finely tuned and highly effective program for pre-marrieds. Dr. Stanley has incorporated Christian principles into the PREP curriculum and formed Christian PREP.

The address and telephone number of both organizations are listed at the end of this appendix. By calling the number you can find out what sort of instructional material is available, and you can also ascertain if there are any certified PREP instructors in your area. It is well worth calling or writing.

I WANT TO COMMUNICATE WITH YOU BECAUSE I LOVE YOU

Good communication begins with the *desire* to communicate properly. It includes an attitude that says, "I want to learn how to express myself to you without becoming abusively angry or hurtful, and I want to listen to you without being overly sensitive or becoming defensive."

If you truly love someone, you want to hear what they have to say, and you want them to hear what *you* have to say. What's more, if you are struggling in this area, there are several study courses and programs that can help you improve, including the PREP program. Let's take a brief look at some of them.

One way to assess your skill as a communicator is to write to Dr. Sherrod Miller, one of the authors of *Talking and Listening Together* (Littleton, CO: Interpersonal Communications, 1991), the workbook for his communications course, and request the "gap" test, a questionnaire for assessing your communication skills and identifying areas that you need to improve. The address and phone number of Dr. Miller's organization, Interpersonal Communication Programs, Inc., are listed at the end of the appendix. This organization has been teaching communication skills for more than twenty-five years, and everything they do is based on years of research. Cindy and I went through a training program conducted by Dr. Miller and were certified as couple communication instructors. It is a program I can recommend without hesitation.

I can also recommend a premarital assessment instrument called PREPARE, which was designed by Dr. David Olsen and contains ten questions designed to assess a couple's communication skills. There are also 115 other questions covering such areas as conflict resolution, personality issues, financial management, leisure activity, sexuality, family and friends, religious orientation, realistic expectations, and children.

Dr. Olsen has been administering and researching the PREPARE instrument since 1980, and his organization, PREPARE/ENRICH Inc. has trained thousands of counselors, pastors, and lay counselors to administer and interpret the information gathered. (The ENRICH half of Dr. Olsen's organization comes from his work to strengthen and improve existing marriages, whereas the PREPARE part is meant for those who are getting ready for marriage.)

There have been at least two major studies that have shown that PREPARE is an effective instrument when it comes to determining which couples will remain happily married and which will wind up in divorce court. Blaine Flowers, who undertook one study, said that after looking at the way the couples responded to PREPARE he was able to predict accurately 86 percent of the time which of those couples would divorce, and 78 percent of the time which couples would still be happily married three years later.

If you want more information write to PREPARE/ENRICH, Inc. at the address at the end of this appendix. You can also get the name of a trained counselor or minister in your zip code who can administer the inventories for you.

I also want to mention a program called Engaged Encounter, which is a spin-off of a larger organization called Marriage Encounter. You've probably heard of Marriage Encounter. It's an organization that has been, for the past twenty-plus years, effectively teaching couples how to communicate through written and verbal dialogue. In the Engaged Encounter program, couples go on a weekend retreat, led by clergy and lay couples, in which they learn some of the principles of a healthy marriage as well as some of the same communication skills and techniques as those taught in the Marriage Encounter program. Once again, an address and phone number is listed in the appendix that can help you contact this organization to see if there are any retreats available in your area.

Finally, I recommend the Premarital Communication Inventory, which was created by Dr. Millard J. Bienvenu. This inventory includes thirty-eight questions which are designed to help dating and/or engaged couples examine and assess their ability to communicate. Dr. Bienvenu's inventory appears in appendix B of this book. There is no right or wrong way to answer these questions. It is not a test to be graded, but rather an instrument to help identify your communication strengths and weaknesses. He has also developed an instrument designed specifically to assess how people communicate anger.

As wise as it is for a person to read all they can on how to communicate more effectively, it is also important to go through the type of training you will receive in such programs as Dr. Markman's PREP or Dr. Miller's Couples Communication Program. Research has shown that simply reading about or listening to lectures regarding communication does not significantly improve one's ability to communicate. There must be hands-on experience, in which you learn communication skills the best way possible—by communicating!

Always remember, all married couples need to learn the art of battle just as they need to learn the art of making love. Good battle is objective and honest—never vicious or cruel. Good battle is healthy and constructive, and brings the principle of equal partnership to a marriage.

The addresses and phone numbers of marital and premarital programs are listed on the following page.

Interpersonal Communication Programs, Inc.
7201 South Broadway, Ste. 11
Littleton, CO 80122
800-328-5099

PREPARE/ENRICH, Inc.
P.O. Box 190
Minneapolis, MN 55440-0190
800-331-1661

Prevention and Relationship Enhancement Program (PREP)
Dr. Howard Markman
Center for Marriage and Family Studies/University of Denver
Denver, CO 80208
303-750-8798

Christian PREP, Inc.
Dr. Scott Stanley
17805 South Bellaire Street, Ste. 621
Denver, CO 80222
To order audiovisual materials from both PREP programs, call
800-366-0166

International Marriage Encounter
955 Lake Street
St. Paul, MN 55120
612-454-6434 (information on materials)

National Marriage Encounter
4704 Jamerson Place
Orlando, FL 32807
800-828-3351 (information on groups)

Family Life Marriage Conferences
3900 North Rodney Parham Rd.
Little Rock, AK 72212
800-358-6329 (information on conferences)

Appendix B

PREMARITAL COMMUNICATION INVENTORY

1. Do you and your fiance discuss your differences?
2. Do you have a tendency to keep your feelings to yourself?
3. Do you and your fiance quarrel very much?
4. Does your fiance tell you when he/she is angry with you?
5. Does he/she stop seeing you without telling you why?
6. Do you ever discuss your views about sex in marriage?
7. Do the two of you settle your disagreements to your satisfaction?
8. Do you find it difficult to talk with your fiance?
9. Do you find his/her voice irritating?
10. Do you discuss your attitudes toward premarital sexual relations?
11. Does your fiance fail to ask your opinion in making plans involving the two of you?
12. Does he/she have a tendency to say things which would be better left unsaid?
13. Do you find it necessary to keep after your fiance for his/her faults?
14. Do you communicate successfully with each other's families?
15. Does it bother you unduly for your fiance to express his/her own beliefs even if they differ from yours?
16. Do you understand his/her feelings and attitudes?

17. Does he/she seem to understand your feelings?
18. Does your fiance nag you?
19. Do you think your fiance is too critical of you?
20. Does your fiance wait until you are through talking before saying what he/she has to say?
21. Do you refrain from saying something when you know it will only hurt your fiance or make matters worse?
22. When a problem arises that needs to be solved are you and your fiance able to discuss it together (in a calm manner)?
23. Is your fiance very jealous of you?
24. Are you very jealous of him/her?
25. Does he/she try to lift your spirits when you're depressed or discouraged?
26. Do you fail to express disagreement with your fiance because you're afraid he/she will get angry?
27. Are you and your fiance able to disagree with one another without losing your tempers?
28. Do you and your fiance discuss how you will manage your money after you're married?
29. Do you have disagreements over money now?
30. Does he/she often say one thing but really mean another?
31. Does your fiance complain that you don't understand him/her?
32. Do you help your fiance to understand you by telling him/her how you think and feel about things?
33. Do the two of you discuss what you expect of one another in terms of a future husband and wife?
34. Does your fiance often sulk and pout?
35. Do you feel that in most matters he/she knows what you are trying to say?
36. Do you discuss your views on rearing children?
37. Do the two of you neglect discussing your religious attitudes and beliefs?

38. Is it easier to confide in a friend than your fiance?

Used by permission of Dr. Millard J. Bienvenu, Ph.D. Copies and a guide for use of this inventory are available. The Inventory of Anger Communication is also available. Call or write:

Millard J. Bienvenu, Ph.D.
Northwest Communications
710 Watson Drive
Natchitoches, LA 71457
318-352-8345

About the Author

A native Texan, David Nicholson, Ph.D., graduated from Vanderbilt University and received his doctorate in clinical psychology from North Texas State University. Before going into private practice he worked for the Minirth Meier New Life Clinic in Richardson, Texas for eight years. A major focus of his current practice is teaching communication and conflict resolution skills to singles groups, married and engaged couples, and businesses. He also conducts video-based parenting seminars for parents of both young children and teenagers.

David and his wife Cindy have been married for eleven years and have three children: Clint, Darcie, and Luke.

If you would like to contact David regarding his seminars or workshops, write to:

Dr. David Nicholson
8340 Meadow
Suite 134
Dallas, TX 75231